BUBBLE AND

SQUEAK

The Leftover Cook Book

By the same author

How To Boil An Egg — Simple Cookery For One

No Meat For Me, Please! — Recipes For The Vegetarian
   In The Family

The Dinner Party Planner

Uniform with this book

BUBBLE AND SQUEAK

The Leftover Cook Book

by

Jan Arkless

PAPERFRONTS
ELLIOT RIGHT WAY BOOKS,
KINGSWOOD, SURREY, U.K.

Typeset in 10pt Times by One & A Half Graphics. Made and Printed in Great Britain by Richard Clay Ltd., Bungay, Suffolk.

This one's for Ki, who
ate up all his "scraps"
and grew the tallest!

CONTENTS

INTRODUCTION

When I decided to write a book on 'Using up Leftovers', I realised I needed to do some market research! So I took the easy option and carried out a straw poll of my friends, neighbours and acquaintances, who all looked slightly bewildered when greeted instead of by 'Hi!' or 'Good Morning', but with 'What do you do with leftovers?'. The answers were amusing and sometimes amazing, ranging from the mundane 'I like bubble and squeak' (apparently the ultimate favourite dish of all the nation's husbands, whether by taste, design or habit I'm still not too sure), to 'I give them to the baby, the dog, the birds, the hedgehog or the cat's visiting ginger boyfriend', to the more exotic ideas, often from people you'd least expect to bother using up stale breadcrumbs in a soufflé (I must ask for that recipe again, I wonder what she really makes!) or whipping up a marvellous pud involving spare egg whites and the remnants of the cake tin.

However, it appears that most people on the whole are thrifty, and don't like to waste anything. Or maybe we're all becoming more and more aware of the need to look after all our resources and recycle everything, including extra food; a lesson to our consciences brought home by the harrowing pictures of famine and deprivation in the Third World sadly so often in the news nowadays.

What's left over seems to vary according to the number in the household — after all, if you're just cooking for one (yourself) it's easy to cook three potatoes if you know that's what you're going to eat, but try cooking for a family of 3, 4 or more — everyone's either starving or slimming: one doesn't have time to eat, has got to dash and will just grab a sandwich; another had a large lunch and only wants a small portion; another doesn't like this dinner anyway and decided this morning to loathe all green vegetables. So one way or another there's often just a little bit of everything left, too small to make a family dinner tomorrow, but it seems wasteful to put it in the bin.

However, often these little bits can be used next day to make a lunch or supper dish for one or two members of the family, or frozen in individual portions to use when someone requires a quick meal or is the only one eating at home that evening. My grown-up family, now mostly away from home, usually raid the freezer before going back to their own flats after a weekend at home: 'just taking something back to make a quick meal, save me shopping tomorrow Mum!'. I suppose we should be glad that we do still cook at home and are not yet as 'take away' minded as they are in the U.S.A. ... I heard a story recently of an American household where, when Mom calls 'dinner's ready', all the kids obediently get into the car ready for the trip to the nearest fast food outlet!

On the other hand, one or two person households often find that they have half a stale loaf or a long-opened bottle of milk lurking in the fridge, as you can't buy really small sizes any more — is there a need to bring back the old half pint milk bottle?

Of course, the big plus of using up leftovers is the feeling of getting something for nothing — rather like the triumphant arrival home with a somewhat squashed plastic bag of hedge-gathered blackberries.

In these health-conscious days do be very careful about storing cooked food or other leftovers — they must always be covered or wrapped to prevent cross-contamination from uncooked foods, such as raw meat or fish (which should also be wrapped), and then put into the fridge, not left lying around in a warm room. Take great care with the re-cooking of leftovers: *the food must be re-cooked properly not just warmed or reheated*. You may need to add extra flavourings to make up for those lost in the second cooking, and always take extra care when storing and re-using gravies and sauces. Don't leave them in the fridge too long before use.

It's a good idea to jazz up leftovers by mixing them with fresh food when possible, but don't fall into the false economy trap of spending excessive amounts on buying fresh ingredients to mix with those two spare egg whites or that small helping of cooked cabbage, unless you're going to produce a dish which everyone will enjoy eating! Of course, you may go to the other extreme and cook extra in order to have some left over on purpose, because everyone wants their favourite leftover dish next day — and once again we're back to the ubiquitous bubble and squeak, or "scraps" as it's known in our family.

In this book I count fresh eggs, cheese, milk and bread as leftovers, although they're not strictly "legit", but most people usually have some in the fridge or larder, which can be used on their own or with genuine leftovers to produce an "instant" meal, to give flavour and texture or to pad out a dish as necessary.

I hope you'll enjoy the suggestions in the recipes, some are very simple variations and memory-joggers of old favourites, others are a bit more unusual or exotic, but they are all tasty and easy to prepare. Because everyone will have different amounts of leftovers, the serving quantities of the recipes vary — some are just for a little amount, some will serve four or six — but they can all be easily adapted to suit your individual requirements. If you haven't got quite enough of all the ingredients in the recipe, experiment and add a bit of whatever you have available — great fun, the only problem being that when someone asks you for the recipe you can never remember exactly what you put in it!

About the recipes

tsp	= teaspoon
dsp	= dessertspoon
tblsp	= tablespoon (serving spoon)
1 spoonful	= 1 slightly rounded spoonful
1 level spoonful	= 1 flat spoonful
1 cupful	= 1 teacup (drinking size cup) approximately ¼ pint/5 fl oz/142ml; *not* the American measure.
mins.	= minutes
pt	= pint

The eggs used in the recipes are size 2 as that is the size I think is best value at my local village shop. The difference between sizes 1, 2 and 3 is very small and will not make much difference in these recipes.

In the recipes, both imperial and metric measurements are given. However, as they are *not* exact conversions you should follow only one set throughout a recipe and not mix the two.

Fan Ovens

Follow the manufacturer's instructions on reducing oven temperatures and cooking times. I have found with my new fan oven that reducing the temperature given in the recipes by about 15-20°C and the cooking times by 5-15 mins. according to the size of the cake or dish (and keeping an eye on the oven and adjusting as necessary!) that the results have been excellent.

1 FISH

Fish is definitely best bought fresh or commercially frozen, and should be cooked and eaten straightaway while as fresh as possible; it isn't wise to leave raw or cooked fish lying around before using it up. I'm sure most people will only buy the amount of fish they need for a particular meal, so generally there will not be fresh fish left over. On the other hand, part of a can of fish, such as tuna or kipper fillets, may be left from when someone has made themselves a sandwich or a snack and left the rest 'for later', which in our house means it moulders away at the back of the fridge until it's put out for the cat, who usually turns her nose up and returns to the 'proper' cat food! However, extra fish can be made into a really tasty meal or snack provided that it is kept covered in the fridge and used as soon as possible (preferably the same day).

Recipes using cooked fish
Chinesey Fried Rice (p. 83)   Quick Kipper Pâté (p. 15)

Salad, Pasta (p. 85)   Salad, Rice (p. 82).
Tuna Continental (see below)

TUNA CONTINENTAL   *Serves 2—4*

Stretches leftover tuna into a lunch for several people, according to amount of tuna and appetites.

Preparation and cooking time: 20 mins.

1 onion
1 clove garlic or ¼ tsp ground garlic
½-1 green pepper
2-3 stalks celery
4 oz/100g mushrooms
1 tblsp oil for frying
1 × 290g can tomato, mushroom or celery soup
4 oz/100g frozen peas or mixed vegetables
Salt, black pepper
½-1 7 oz/198g size can tuna fish
To serve: **plain boiled rice — allow approx. 2 oz/50g**
uncooked rice per person or 1 cup cooked rice
each, reheated in the microwave (follow the
instructions for your model)
Lemon wedges and parsley for garnish

Put rice on to cook in a pan of boiling salted water, allowing 10-15 mins. for white rice, 20-25 mins. for brown rice, or as directed on the packet.

Peel and chop onion, peel and crush fresh garlic. Wash and chop pepper and celery, slice mushrooms. Heat oil in a pan over a moderate heat and fry onion with garlic for 2-3 mins., until beginning to soften. Add pepper and celery and fry for a further 4-5 mins., then stir in sliced mushrooms and cook for another minute or two until just soft. Stir in chosen soup, stir in peas or mixed vegetables (these can be cooked from frozen), and cook for a further 3-5 mins. until sauce is hot, thick and tasty. Season to taste and stir in tuna, being careful not to break it up too small. Heat thoroughly over a low heat, stirring very gently.

Drain rice and arrange in a ring on a serving dish. Pour tuna sauce into the ring and serve hot, garnished with a little fresh snipped parsley and lemon wedges.

QUICK KIPPER PÂTÉ
Serves 1 or 2

This isn't really a pâté recipe, more a kind of posh spread. It's a delicious way to use up that half packet of defrosted kipper fillets left by 'someone' who only wanted one or two fillets for a quick snack earlier in the day!

Preparation time: 10 mins. plus chilling time if possible

½-1 170g size packet cooked kipper fillets
1-2 oz/25-50g butter (nicer than margarine!)
1-2 tsp lemon juice
Salt, black pepper
Pinch cayenne pepper, pinch nutmeg (optional)
Handful fresh cloves or 2 or 3 spring onions (optional)

Cook fish (if not already cooked) according to instructions on packet. Remove and discard any skin or stray bones from fish. Put the fish into a basin, and mash it well with a fork. Soften the butter (but don't melt it), and beat enough butter into the fish to make a soft pâté. Season well with lemon juice, salt, pepper and spices, and stir in a few washed, finely snipped chives or chopped spring onions if liked. Spoon into 1 or 2 little ramekin dishes, cover with plastic film and chill in fridge until needed.

Serve with fresh brown bread and butter, granary rolls or French bread.

If you are lucky enough to have any smoked salmon 'lying

about' — perhaps the last scraps from a piece you had at Christmas — these can be mashed in with the kipper fillets or used on their own if you have enough.

For a change of flavour, mix the mashed fish with cream cheese instead of, or mixed with, the softened butter.

2 MEAT & POULTRY

Nowadays people don't seem to have so much meat left over — for one thing we are buying and eating less meat for both health and humanitarian reasons, and it's far too expensive to waste. We now tend to buy smaller joints to last one or two meals at the most, buying different food for the rest of the week (the exception to this being Christmas). The old traditional 'cold meat and boiled potato' Monday dinner followed on Tuesday by Shepherd's Pie made with the minced remains of the Sunday joint went out with the advent of the automatic washing machine and the end of the traditional weekly Monday washday.

Don't waste beautiful cold roast meats always trying to think of something clever to make with them — what's wrong with cold beef, chips and pickles, with a crisp salad on the side; a lovely thick cold pork, stuffing and apple sauce sandwich in fresh granary bread; or cold lamb with mint sauce, new potatoes and peas with some tasty gravy?

Rechauffé or recooked meat needs plenty of extra sauces and flavourings to 'pep it up', as flavour is lost during the recooking process. There are lots of tasty sauces readily available — tomato ketchup, Worcester and soy sauces, brown sauces and pickles and chutneys, stock cubes in various flavours and, of course, all sorts of fresh and dried herbs and spices — so that it's easy to give a really interesting or intriguing taste to a dish. Be careful though, don't get carried away, add a little bit at a time and taste as you go!

Food Hygiene

For goodness' sake, be careful how you store cooked meat and meat products — there have been so many awful scares about food poisoning lately. Always store cooked meat in the fridge and remember to put the half carved joint or carcass into the fridge straight after the meal — don't leave it standing around in the warm kitchen while you have your pudding, coffee and afternoon snooze, or worse still, leave it overnight after a late dinner party. All cooked meats should be covered or wrapped and stored in the fridge, away from any raw meat (which should also be wrapped so that bacteria are not passed from fresh to cooked food). In shops, raw and cooked meats are not allowed to be kept in the same compartment, so do take care in your own fridge.

Make sure, too, that when the meat is reheated it is recooked right through; *never* serve meat that is just rewarmed. And always remember — if in doubt about whether something is still fresh, bin it!! It's better to waste a few slices of turkey than have everyone ill. On the other hand, as long as you're sensible, cooked meat and other leftovers can be made into completely safe, delicious meals which everyone can enjoy.

Recipes using bacon rashers (uncooked)

Soups: General Vegetable (p. 62)
       (Cheating Mulligatawnyish — p. 66
       Minestrone Mixture — p. 65
       Thick Vegetable & Lentil — p. 65)

Recipes using cooked beef

Cheating Chop Suey (p. 38)   Curry, Meat (p. 25)
Moorland Pasties (p. 22)   Stuffed Peppers (p. 28)

Recipes using cooked beef which needs mincing/processing

Beefy Bullets (p. 25)   Crispy Shepherd's Pie
Harvest Festival Special   (p. 28)
  (p. 23)   Meat Patacakes (p. 22)
Monday Moussaka (p. 34)   Old Fashioned Potted Beef
Savoury Potato Nests (p. 26) (p. 32)

Recipe using Bolognese sauce

Quick Savoury Pancakes (p. 30)

Recipes using cooked chicken/turkey

Charlbury Chow Mein   Cheating Chop Suey
  (p. 40)   (p. 38)
Chicken & Ham Gougère   Chinese Chicken
  (p. 50)   (p. 45)
Chinesey Fried Rice (p. 83) Christmas Pie (p. 37)
Creamed Chicken Mornay   Curry, Meat (p. 25)
  (p. 52)   Egg Tortilla (p. 89)
Moorland Pasties (p. 22)   Mousse, Posh Chicken or
Quiche Lorraine (p. 91)   Turkey (p. 49)
Risotto (p. 44)   Salad, Boxing Day (p. 48)
Salad, Pasta (p. 85)   Salad, Rice (p. 82)
Savoury Flan (p. 79)   Soup, Tim's Cream of Turkey
Stuffed Peppers (p. 28)   or Chicken (p. 41)

Recipes using cooked chicken/turkey which needs mincing/processing

Beefy Bullets (p. 25)

Harvest Festival Special (p. 23)

Savoury Potato Nests (p. 26)

Crispy Shepherd's Pie (p. 28)

Meat Patacakes (p. 22)

Spanish Turkey or Chicken (p. 47)

Recipes using gravy

Chinese Chicken (p. 45)

Crispy Shepherd's Pie (p. 28)

Monday Special (p. 67)

Savoury Potato Nests (p. 26)

Stuffed Peppers (p. 28)

Vegetable Crumble (p. 72)

Christmas Pie (p. 37)

Minted Lamb Slices (p. 33)

Monday Moussaka (p. 34)

Risotto (p. 44)

Soups (p. 41, p. 62, p. 65)

Recipes using cooked ham

Chicken & Ham Gougère (p. 50)

Egg Tortilla (p. 89)

Moorland Pasties (p. 22)

Risotto (p. 44)

Salad, Rice (p. 82)

Stuffed Peppers (p. 28)

Chinesey Fried Rice (p. 83)

Christmas Pie (p. 37)

Ham & Egg Pie (p. 52)

Quiche Lorraine (p. 91)

Salad, Pasta (p. 85)

Savoury Flan (p. 79)

Recipes using cooked ham which needs mincing/processing

Beefy Bullets (p. 25)

Harvest Festival Special (p. 23)

Crispy Shepherd's Pie (p. 28)

Meat Patacakes (p. 22)

Savoury Potato Nests (p. 26)

Recipes using cooked lamb

Curry, Meat (p. 25)
Minted Lamb Slices (p. 33)
Moorland Pasties (p. 22)
Greek-style Stuffed
  Aubergines (p. 35)
Stuffed Peppers (p. 28)

Recipes using cooked lamb which needs mincing/processing

Beefy Bullets (p. 25)
Harvest Festival Special
  (p. 23)
Monday Moussaka (p.34)
Crispy Shepherd's Pie
  (p. 28)
Meat Patacakes (p. 22)
Savoury Potato Nests (p. 26)

Recipes using cooked pork

Charlbury Chow Mein
  (p. 40)
Christmas Pie (p. 37)
Stuffed Peppers (p. 28)
Cheating Chop
  Suey (p. 38)
Moorland Pasties
  (p. 22)

Recipes using cooked pork which needs mincing/processing

Beefy Bullets (p. 25)
Harvest Festival Special
  (p. 23)
Savoury Potato Nests
  (p. 26)
Crispy Shepherd's Pie
  (p. 28)
Meat Patacakes (p. 22)

Recipes using raw sausages/sausagemeat

Sausage Rolls, Cheese Pastry (p. 111)
Toad in the Hole (p. 31)

Recipes using cooked sausages/sausagemeat

Egg Tortilla (p. 89)   Salad, Pasta (p. 85)

MEAT PATACAKES
Makes 8 cakes

Use up cold cooked potatoes as well as cold meat, or cook and mash some fresh potatoes. These make a quick, economical high tea or supper dish. A food processor is useful for this recipe.

Preparation and cooking time: 15 mins.

1 lb/500g cooked mashed potato
¾ lb/375g cooked meat — beef, lamb, pork, poultry or ham
1 medium onion
1 egg
Salt, pepper
1 tsp mixed herbs and/or few sprigs fresh parsley or chives
Little flour for shaping
2-3 tblsp oil for frying

Mash potatoes thoroughly and beat until smooth.

Remove any fat or gristle from meat and mince finely or process in a processor. Peel and mince or grate onion. Stir meat and onion into potato and mix together with enough beaten egg to form a stiff mixture. Season with salt, pepper, dried or finely snipped fresh herbs.

Turn onto a lightly floured board, divide into 8 equal pieces and shape into round patacakes, using your hand and a palette knife. Heat oil for frying in a frying pan over a moderate heat, and fry patacakes for 2-3 mins. on each side until golden brown. Drain well on kitchen paper and serve hot with a crisp salad or baked beans according to taste.

MOORLAND PASTIES
Makes 4

A quickly cooked meat and vegetable pastry, filled with whatever's left in the fridge. Tasty hot or cold.

Preparation and cooking time: 40-45 mins.

8 oz/250g homemade or bought shortcrust pastry
4 oz/125g cooked meat — beef, lamb, pork, poultry or ham
1 medium onion
2 medium-sized cooked potatoes
3-4 tblsp cooked mixed vegetables — carrots, swede,
**   peas, cauliflower, broccoli, etc.**
Salt, pepper, mixed herbs
Dash of Worcester sauce or 1 tblsp pickle or chutney
**   (optional)**
1 tblsp gravy, brown sauce or tomato ketchup for mixing
Little milk for brushing

Heat oven to 200°C/400°F/gas 6-7.

Roll pastry out approx. ¼"/½cm thick and cut out 4 rounds using a large saucer or teaplate.

Chop or mince meat and put into a bowl. Chop finely or mince onion and add to meat. Dice potatoes, chop vegetables (not too small), and stir into meat mixture. Season well adding herbs, pickles and sauces to taste, adding a little gravy if necessary to bind mixture together.

Divide filling between pastry rounds, brush edges with milk and bring pastry edges together to form pasties. Press tightly to seal and flute edges. Put onto a baking sheet, brush with milk and prick steam holes on each side. Bake for 20 mins. until pastry is lightly browned, reducing oven heat after 10 mins. to 180°C/350°F/gas 4-5 if the pastry seems to be getting too brown (you must allow time to cook the filling thoroughly, not just warm it through).

Serve hot or cold; good as part of a main meal or in a packed lunch.

HARVEST FESTIVAL SPECIAL   *Serves 4*

Although you can use one of the giant Harvest Festival size marrows for this, you'd need a huge dish and a very large family to eat it. A smaller, young marrow is plenty for four people and has more taste. A food processor is useful for this recipe.

Preparation and cooking time: 1¾-2 hours.

1 small-medium sized marrow
1 lb/500g cooked meat — beef, pork, lamb, poultry or ham
1 small onion
1 tblsp oil and 1 oz (25g) butter for frying
1-2 tblsp stuffing mix (I like country stuffing with beef; sage and onion with pork; thyme and parsley with lamb or poultry)
1 tsp mixed dried herbs and a few sprigs fresh parsley
Little water, stock, wine or cider
Topping: **1-2 slices brown or granary bread**
1 oz/25g butter

Heat oven to 180°C/350°F/gas 4-5.

Peel marrow, cut in half lengthways, making the top 'half' smaller to form a lid. Scoop out seeds to form a hollow. Mince cooked meat or put through a food processor. Peel and finely chop onion. Heat oil in a pan over a moderate heat, add onion and fry gently for 3-4 mins. until soft but not brown. Stir in meat, stuffing mix, herbs and seasoning, adding a little chosen liquid as required to make a soft stuffing mix. Fill hollow in marrow with stuffing, piling it up well, and cover with the hollow marrow lid. Place in a large, well-greased casserole or oven-proof dish, dot with butter and cover with a lid or piece of kitchen foil. Bake in the moderate oven for about 1 hour, basting occasionally with the buttery juices.

While marrow is cooking, make breadcrumbs. Heat butter and oil in a frying pan and fry breadcrumbs for 2-3 mins. until crisp.

Increase oven heat to 200°C/400°F/gas 6-7. Remove lid from marrow, baste again, then carefully sprinkle with the crispy crumbs. Return marrow to the oven and bake for a further 15-20 mins. until topping is golden brown. This is nice served with homemade or bought tomato sauce or a spicy gravy.

MEAT CURRY

Serves 4

Use up any cooked meat by serving it in a spicy curry sauce.

Preparation and cooking time: 1 hour

Curry sauce — see page 70
1 lb/500g cooked beef, lamb, turkey or chicken
Cooked vegetables (as for vegetable curry, if you have any
to use, but these are optional)

Cut chosen meat into large dice or slice into bite-sized pieces. Cut vegetables into pieces, if used. Prepare curry sauce, and when it is thick stir in the meat and simmer very gently for 10-15 mins., until the meat is thoroughly reheated and has absorbed the lovely flavours from the curry sauce. Add any cooked vegetables for the last 5-10 mins. of cooking time and make sure everything is piping hot. Serve with poppadums and side dishes as for vegetable curry.

BEEFY BULLETS

Makes 6-8

Makes an economical change from beefburgers as a small amount of meat goes a long way. Serve with chips and beans, or new potatoes and a crisp green vegetable for more sophisticated tastes. A food processor is useful for this recipe.

Preparation and cooking time: 20-25 mins.

½ lb/250g cooked beef (you can use lamb, pork, poultry or
ham if you prefer, and make meaty bullets)
1 oz/25g butter or margarine
1 oz/25g cornflour or flour
¼ pt/150ml milk or stock

(continued overleaf)

(Beefy Bullets continued)

Salt, pepper, shake of cayenne pepper (optional)
Dash of sauce to flavour — Worcester, soy, brown or tomato
Few sprigs fresh parsley
Coating: **1 egg**
         3 tblsp dried breadcrumbs, homemade or bought
Deep fat for frying

Remove any fat or gristle from meat and mince or process.

Make a thick sauce — melt butter or margarine in a pan over a moderate heat, add cornflour or flour and stir to thicken. Gradually stir in chosen liquid and beat well over the heat to make a thick, smooth sauce. Add the minced meat and season to taste with salt, peppers, sauce and fresh finely snipped parsley.

Divide mixture into 6-8 equal-sized portions and roll into bullet-shaped croquets (if mixture is too soft, cool it in fridge or freezer for a few minutes until firm). Beat egg for coating and pour into a shallow dish. Pour crumbs onto a plate. Dip bullets into the egg, then roll them in the crumbs. Repeat to form a thin coating.

Heat fat in deep fryer to maker's recommended temperature, (usually 170-180°C/350-375°F) and fry bullets in the deep fat for 3-5 mins., shaking occasionally to fry evenly, until crisp and golden brown. Or shallow fry in a little fat in a frying pan for 4-5 mins., turning several times to cook evenly. Drain well on kitchen paper and serve hot with chosen accompaniments.

SAVOURY POTATO NESTS   *Serves 3-4*

Use either cold meat, minced or processed, and mixed with leftover gravy, or pre-cooked mince. (I save time when cooking mince by making double quantity and freezing half for future meals.) You can also use up cold mashed potato for the flan, adding extra freshly cooked potato as necessary.

Preparation and cooking time: 30-40 mins.

1-1½ lb/500g cooked mashed potato — enough for your family
1 oz/25g butter or margarine
1 egg or 1 egg yolk and a little milk
¾-1 lb/350-500g cold cooked meat (minced, processed or chopped) or 1 lb/500g cooked mince
½ pt/300ml approx. gravy
Seasoning to taste: **salt, pepper, Worcester, soy or brown sauce, tabasco, tomato ketchup, etc.**
1-2 tsp chopped mixed herbs, dried or fresh
Garnish: **1-2 tomatoes, fresh parsley**

Heat oven to 200°C/400°F/ gas 6-7.

Mash potatoes (mix cold potatoes with freshly cooked boiled potato if you didn't have enough leftover), mix in melted butter or margarine and enough beaten egg and/or milk to make a thick, smooth mixture, beating well with an electric mixer or wooden spoon. Grease a baking tray well and pipe or spoon 3 or 4 potato nests, or grease well a loose-based deep sandwich cake tin and line the base and sides with potato to make a large nest (the potato lining should be approx. 1"/2½cm thick). Brush nests with beaten egg or milk and bake in the hot oven for 10 mins. (small nests), 15 mins. (large nest) until golden brown and crispy on the outside. Warm serving plates.

While nests are cooking, mix chosen minced meat, gravy and seasonings in a saucepan, bring to the boil over a moderate heat, reduce heat and simmer for 5-10 mins. until meat and sauce are thoroughly recooked and piping hot. Taste and adjust seasoning as needed.

Carefully turn hot potato nests onto serving plates and fill with the hot meat mixture. Garnish with tomato wedges and parsley and serve at once.

To save time, the potato nest can be made in a very well-greased oven-proof dish and forked into shape. Fill the uncooked nest with the cold but seasoned meat mixture, then bake in the hot oven for 20-25 mins. until thoroughly hot and bubbling right through. Garnish as before and serve at once.

CRISPY SHEPHERD'S PIE   *Serves 3-4*

Use the recipe for Savoury Potato Nests (page 26), adding a crispy cheese topping.

Preparation and cooking time: 35-40 mins.

Meat mixture and creamed potato as given on page 27
Crispy topping: **2 oz/50g grated Cheddar cheese**
              1 thick slice or 1 roll granary or seed bread

Heat oven to 200°C/400°F/gas 6-7.
    Prepare creamed potatoes as for Savoury Potato Nests.
    Prepare chosen meat mixture as before but do not heat, and use less gravy, approx. 1 cup/¼ pt/150ml to make a stiffer mixture. Put cold meat mixture into a 2½ pt/1 litre pie dish or deep oven-proof dish, spoon creamed potato mixture on top of meat and fork down neatly. Grate cheese (use up small leftover pieces), make bread into breadcrumbs, mix them together and sprinkle over pie. Dot with butter and bake in the hot oven for 20-25 mins. until topping is crispy and golden and the meat mixture is completely recooked. Serve hot, garnished with tomato slices, fresh parsley or watercress.
    Individual pies can be made in little dishes or foil containers and the pies baked for 15-20 mins.

STUFFED PEPPERS   *Serves 4*

A very pretty dish for lunch or supper. Use all green peppers or serve a different colour — red, yellow, orange, green — to each member of the family. Any good quality cold cooked meat can be used with appropriate 'flavour' gravy or soup. A food processor is useful for this recipe.

Preparation and cooking time: 1 hour

4 sweet peppers — colours of choice
6-8 oz/150-250g cold, cooked meat — lamb, beef, pork, poultry or ham
1 onion
1-2 cloves garlic (optional)
1-2 tblsp oil for frying
4 oz/100g/1 cup cold cooked rice
1-2 tomatoes — you can use the squashy ones or 'cooking' tomatoes
1 tblsp tomato purée (optional)
2-3 tblsp gravy or soup (I like gravy with lamb and beef, chicken soup with ham, and mushroom soup with poultry)
Salt, pepper
1-2 tsp dried herbs to taste — mixed herbs, oregano, basil, etc.
Few sprigs fresh parsley

Heat oven to 180°C/350°F/gas 4-5.

Wash peppers, cut off tops to make lids. Core and seed pepper shells. Put peppers and tops into a pan of water, bring to the boil and simmer for 2-3 mins. to soften slightly. Drain well and put aside.

Remove any fat or gristle from meat and process or chop finely. Peel and finely chop onion and garlic. Heat oil in a pan over moderate heat and fry onion and garlic for 3-4 mins. until soft. Remove from heat and stir in chopped meat, rice and tomatoes. Bind together with tomato purée if used, gravy or soup, and season well with salt, pepper and chosen herbs, including a little fresh snipped parsley if available.

Fill pepper shells with the mixture, top with the lids, and place in a well-greased oven-proof dish. Cover with a lid or piece of cooking foil and bake in the moderate oven for 35-40 mins. until peppers are cooked.

This recipe can also be used as a starter, allowing half a pepper per serving. Cut the peppers in half vertically and blanch as before. Fill pepper halves with stuffing, place in the greased dish, cover with a lid, and bake for 20-25 mins. until soft. Serve garnished with a little salad or bunches of watercress. Different coloured peppers look most attractive cooked in this way.

QUICK SAVOURY PANCAKES   *6-8 pancakes*

Use up any leftover Bolognese or chilli sauce for a quick supper dish.

Preparation and cooking time: 30 mins.

Pancake batter:	**4 oz/100g plain flour**
	Pinch salt
	1 egg
	½ pt/300ml milk
	2-3 tblsp oil for frying
Filling:	**½ pt/300ml/2 cups cooked Bolognese or chilli sauce**
	½ pt/300ml/2 cups homemade or bought tomato sauce
	(use the sauces you can buy for casseroles)

Parsley or watercress for garnish

Make pancakes — mix flour and salt, beat in egg and gradually beat in milk to make a thin batter. Heat a little oil in an omelette or frying pan, and when hot pour in enough batter just to cover the base thinly. Cook for 1-2 mins. until firm, then toss or turn and cook other side. Slide onto a plate and keep warm in a low oven, 100°C/200°F/gas 1, and fry remaining pancakes.

Put chosen Bolognese or chilli sauce into a saucepan and heat gently until piping hot, cooking right through not just warming up. Put hot pancakes onto clean worktop and divide hot filling between them. Roll up pancakes and place on a hot serving dish in the warm oven. Heat chosen tomato sauce in the saucepan and when really hot pour over pancakes. Garnish with parsley or watercress and serve.

TOAD IN THE HOLE   *Serves 2-4*

Use up extra milk in the pancake batter and make a few sausages into a complete meal.

Preparation and cooking time: 45-60 mins.

½ pt/300ml pancake batter — see Quick Savoury Pancakes, opposite
½-1 lb/250-500g sausages (chipolatas or thick ones)
2-3 tblsp dripping or cooking oil

Heat oven to 200°C/400°F/gas 6-7.

Make batter. Prick sausages. Put dripping or oil into a shallow baking tin (large enough to hold all the sausages), and arrange sausages inside. Put into the hot oven and cook for 5-10 mins. until hot and sizzling. Remove tin from oven, turn sausages over and pour the batter over the top. Return pan to oven, and cook for a further 15-20 mins. (small sausages) or 20-30 mins. (large sausages), until batter is puffy, crisp and golden brown. Serve at once, with a tasty gravy and vegetables, or baked beans.

TADPOLES   *Serves 2-4*

These are tiny 'Toad in the Holes'.

Preparation and cooking time: 30 mins.

½ pt/300ml pancake batter — see Quick Savoury Pancakes,
   page 30
½ lb/250g sausage meat, chipolatas or large sausages or
   ½ pt/300ml/2 cups cooked Bolognese or chilli sauce
2-3 tblsp dripping or vegetable oil

Heat oven to 200°C/400°F/gas 6-7.
   Make batter as on page 30.
   Put a little dripping or oil into 8-12 patty or bun tins
(according to size), and put a lump of sausage meat or piece of
sausage in each. Put into the hot oven for 4-5 mins. until fat is
hot and sizzling. Remove tin from oven, pour batter over the top
of sausage and return to the oven for a further 15-20 mins., until
the pop overs have popped up and are puffy, crisp and golden.
   Eat at once, with veg. and gravy or beans, as for Toad in
the Hole.

OLD FASHIONED POTTED BEEF   *Serves 2-3*

A tasty spread for lunch or supper, very good with crusty French
bread, warm brown rolls or hot toast. Makes a satisfying
sandwich filling too, with lettuce, tomato and cucumber. A food
processor is useful for this recipe.

Preparation time: 15 mins.

4 oz/100g butter
8 oz/200g cooked beef
Salt, pepper, nutmeg or mixed spice
Shake of cayenne or paprika pepper to taste
½-1 tsp French or English mustard or horseradish sauce
   (optional)

1 tsp fresh finely chopped or dried herbs — parsley, chives, spring onion tops as available

Clarify butter — cut into pieces, put into a pan and melt slowly over a low heat; do not allow it to boil or brown. When butter is a hot liquid just below boiling point, carefully pour off the clear golden liquid into a heat-proof jug, leaving the white sediment behind in the saucepan.

Remove any fat or gristle from beef, then pass it through a food processor or mince finely 2 or 3 times and pound into a smooth paste with a pestle or a wooden spoon. Season to taste with salt, pepper and chosen spices, sauces and herbs. Press into 2 or 3 ramekins or small pots and smooth tops. Pour clarified butter over each pot to make a thin lid. Leave to set in the fridge and eat the same day.

MINTED LAMB SLICES   *Serves 2-3*

A tasty way of using up cold lamb from the Sunday joint. Serve with roast, creamed or new potatoes and freshly cooked vegetables. If you don't have any leftover gravy use a can of condensed soup.

Preparation and cooking time: 30 mins.

½ lb/250g sliced cold lamb
2-3 tblsp thick mint sauce
½ pt/300ml approx. gravy or condensed oxtail soup (thinned with a little water, wine or cider)

Heat oven to 200°C/400°F/gas 6-7.

Arrange meat slices in a shallow oven-proof dish. Sprinkle slices with the thick mint sauce. Heat gravy or soup in a saucepan with a little chosen liquid if needed to make a thick pouring

sauce, and pour the hot sauce over the meat. Cover with a lid
or piece of cooking foil, and cook in the hot oven for 15 mins.
until meat and sauce are heated right through. If serving with
roast potatoes, put meat in the oven on the lower shelf for the
last 15-20 mins. of their cooking time.

MONDAY MOUSSAKA   *Serves 4*

A lovely garlicky dish which may remind you of summer
holidays spent abroad. Traditionally moussaka is made with
lamb, but is perfectly acceptable with minced beef. A food
processor is useful for this recipe.

Preparation and cooking time: 50-55 mins.

1 lb/500g cooked lamb
1-2 onions
2-3 cloves garlic (optional)
2-3 aubergines — according to size
3-4 tblsp oil for frying
1 tblsp tomato purée
2-3 tblsp stock, gravy or tomato juice from the can
Salt, pepper
1 tsp mixed dried herbs and/or ½ tsp dried oregano
½ lb/250g fresh tomatoes (you can use up the squashy ones)
    or use a drained 14 oz/397g can tomatoes

Quick cheese sauce: 2 heaped tblsp cornflour or flour
                       ½ pt/300ml milk
                       1 oz/25g butter or margarine
                       4 oz/100g grated Cheddar cheese
                       ½ tsp mustard, salt, pepper
                       1 beaten egg
1 heaped tblsp grated Parmesan cheese

Heat oven to 180°C/350°F/gas 4-5.

Mince or process lamb. Peel and chop onions and garlic. Trim, wash and slice aubergines. Heat 1 tblsp oil in a large frying pan over a moderate heat and fry onions and garlic for 2-3 mins. until softened but not brown. Add minced meat and continue to fry, stirring well, for a further 3-4 mins. until meat is browned. Add tomato purée and chosen liquid and season to taste. Put into a deep 3 pt/1¾ litre oven-proof dish and put to one side.

Add more oil to the pan and fry aubergine slices over a moderate heat for 4-5 mins., turning to colour both sides (you may have to cook the slices a few at a time as they take up a lot of room in the pan). Arrange cooked aubergine on top of the meat.

Slice fresh tomatoes or drain canned ones, and soften in the frying pan for 1-2 mins., adding a little more oil if needed. Pour tomatoes and juices on top of aubergines.

Make quick cheese sauce — put cornflour or flour into a basin and mix to a runny paste with a little of the milk. Heat rest of milk and pour onto flour mixture, stirring well. Pour mixture back into pan and reheat, stirring all the time until mixture thickens. Beat in butter or margarine and grated cheese, and season with salt, pepper and mustard. Cool slightly and beat in egg. Pour sauce over meat and vegetables in dish, sprinkle with Parmesan cheese and bake in the moderate oven for 25-30 mins. until piping hot with a lovely golden bubbly top.

Serve with green salad and brown bread rolls (or hot garlic bread if you want to be very self indulgent!).

GREEK-STYLE STUFFED AUBERGINES

Serves 2-4

Allow a whole aubergine per person for a main meal, served with vegetables or salad, or serve half an aubergine each for a substantial and unusual starter. A food processor is useful for this recipe.

Preparation and cooking time: 35 mins., plus 30 mins. draining time

2-4 medium-sized aubergines

For each aubergine allow:
1 oz/25g butter and 1 tsp olive oil
½ small onion
1 clove garlic
1 tomato (squashy ones are fine)
2 oz/50g cooked lamb
1 tsp lemon juice
Salt, black pepper, cayenne pepper (optional)
¼ tsp mixed herbs, pinch oregano and/or basil, sprig parsley
1 tsp grated Parmesan cheese

Wash aubergines, cut in half lengthwise. Loosen flesh from sides of skin and cut across flesh several times. Sprinkle with salt and place cut-side-down in a colander over a plate. Leave to drain for 20-30 mins. to get rid of the bitter juices.

Heat oven to 200°C/400°F/gas 6-7.

Rinse and dry aubergines, arrange cut-side-up in a greased oven-proof dish, dot with half the butter, cover with a lid or cooking foil and bake for 15-20 mins. until soft.

Meanwhile, peel and finely chop onion and garlic and wash and chop tomato. Mince, process or finely chop lamb. Heat remaining butter with the olive oil in a pan over a moderate heat and fry onion and garlic for 3-4 mins. until soft. Add chopped tomato and cook for a further 2-3 mins. Stir in minced lamb, season to taste with lemon juice, salt, pepper, and herbs and heat gently until mixture is hot.

Take aubergines from oven and allow to cool slightly. Then carefully scoop cooked aubergine from the centres, leaving enough flesh to make a firm case. Dice aubergine and stir into hot meat mixture. Adjust seasoning. Pile hot stuffing into aubergine cases, sprinkle with grated Parmesan cheese and reheat in the hot oven for 5-10 mins. until golden and bubbling.

You can use minced beef for this recipe (as long as you don't serve it to a traditional Greek cook!).

CHRISTMAS PIE

Serves 4-6

I called this Pork and Apple Pie until Gladys, my invaluable helper, told me about a delicious Christmas Pie that her daughter makes every year, which seems a far more appropriate title as you can use cooked pork, ham or poultry or a mixture as available.

Preparation and cooking time: 1 hour.

1 lb/500g approx. cooked meat — any mixture as above
2 onions
2 medium-sized cooking apples or 3-4 tblsp apple sauce
2 medium-sized boiled potatoes
3-4 tblsp cooked stuffing (if available)
2-3 tblsp cranberry sauce (optional)
1 tsp dried mixed herbs (use 2 tsp if not adding stuffing)
½ tsp dried thyme, ½ tsp dried sage
Few sprigs fresh parsley
Salt, black pepper
¼ pt/150ml/1 cup approx. gravy or stock
8 oz/225g shortcrust pastry (homemade or bought) or puff
   pastry if preferred
Milk for brushing

Heat oven to 200°C/400°F/gas 6-7.

Remove any fat or gristle from meat and cut into chunks. Peel and chop onions finely; peel, core and dice apples; cut potatoes into chunks; crumble stuffing. Put a layer of meat into a

2½ pt/1¼ litre pie dish, cover with a layer of potato, onion, apple and stuffing, dot with cranberry sauce and sprinkle with dried herbs, snipped parsley, salt and pepper. Repeat layers until all the filling is used up. Pour stock or gravy over filling.

Roll out pastry and cover pie filling, fluting down edges and decorating top of pie with pastry leaves. Brush pie crust with milk and cut a tiny air hole in the centre of crust. Bake in the hot oven for 25-35 mins., lowering heat to 180°C/350°F/gas 4-5 if crust gets too brown before filling is cooked.

Serve hot with vegetables or cold with salad.

If the pie is to be eaten cold as part of a picnic or packed lunch, it is easier to carry if cooked in a shallow tin (a sandwich cake tin for instance) with pastry underneath the filling as well as on top. Line the tin with thinly rolled shortcrust pastry, layer the filling as before, and cover with a thin pastry crust, pinching the edges together well. Bake in the hot oven as above, until pastry is crisp and golden.

If you're a keen pie maker, this filling can be used with hot water crust pastry to make a raised pie.

CHEATING CHOP SUEY   *Serves 4*

This is usually made with raw meat but it works well with cooked pork or poultry. Use less meat and add more vegetables according to availability or whatever you have left in the fridge. It is best to stir fry with raw veg., but you can mix in some cooked ones if you want to use them up. Get all the ingredients sliced and prepared in advance, as the actual stir fry cooking time is very quick.

Preparation and cooking time: 15 mins. plus 30 mins. soaking time

8 oz/250g cooked pork (or beef or poultry)
Marinade: **2 heaped tsp cornflour**
          2 tblsp soy sauce

1 tblsp dry sherry
2 tsp sugar
Dash tabasco or Worcester sauce (optional)

Use a mixture of veg. as available, but try to get a good variety of types, shapes and textures. Choose from the following suggestions:

4 oz/100g fresh beansprouts
4 spring onions and/or 1 small onion
½ small red and/or ½ small green pepper
2-3 small carrots
2-3 tomatoes
Few broccoli or cauliflower florets
2 oz/50g mushrooms
Few green beans
1 small courgette
Small piece root ginger (optional)
1-2 cloves garlic
4-5 tblsp oil for frying
Salt, black pepper

Remove fat and gristle from meat, cut into thin slices and then into strips. Mix marinade, stir in meat and leave for 30 mins., stirring occasionally (if you're short of time, just soak while preparing veg.).

Prepare chosen vegetables: Wash beansprouts in cold water, drain well. Trim and wash spring onions, cut into 2″/5cm strips; peel and very thinly slice onion. Wash, core and de-seed peppers, cut into small chunks or strips. Wash and peel carrots, cut into thin rings or matchsticks. Wash tomatoes, cut into quarters or eighths. Wash broccoli or cauliflower, cut into small separate florets. Wash and slice mushrooms. Top, tail and slice green beans. Wash, top and tail courgette, cut into thin rounds or matchsticks. Peel and finely chop root ginger. Peel and crush or finely chop garlic.

Heat 2-3 tblsp oil in a wok or large frying pan. Remove meat from marinade with a slotted spoon and fry meat in the hot oil for a few moments, stirring and turning to heat right through. Remove from pan and put aside. Add more oil to pan, stir in onion, garlic and ginger and stir fry for 1-2 mins. until softened. Gradually add rest of prepared vegetables and fry for a further 2-3 mins. until all the vegetables are cooked and hot, but still crisp and crunchy. Stir in the fried meat, pour over the rest of the marinade and cook for a moment until everything is hot and the sauce has thickened. Serve with boiled rice.

CHARLBURY CHOW MEIN   *Serves 4*

We've no Chinese take away in Charlbury, so we have to make our own! A quickly prepared, cheap meal, making a little meat go a long way, and far more adventurous than cold meat and chips.

Preparation and cooking time: 20-25 mins.

8 oz/225g dry uncooked egg noodles or tagliatelle (you can use up leftover cooked noodles if you have them)
8 oz/225g cooked pork or poultry
1 tsp cornflour
1 small onion
2″/5cm chunk cucumber
1 × 250g can Chinese stir fry vegetables
4-5 tblsp oil for frying

Sauce: **1 tsp cornflour**
        2 tblsp soy sauce
        1 tblsp dry sherry
        1 tsp sugar
        Salt, black pepper

Cook noodles in boiling salted water for 5-6 mins., until cooked *al dente,* not soft and sticky. Drain well, rinse in cold water and drain again.

Cut meat into thick matchsticks and toss in a basin with the cornflour. Peel and thinly slice onion, cut cucumber into matchsticks, well drain stir fry vegetables.

Mix sauce ingredients to a runny paste in a small basin. Heat half the oil in a wok or frying pan, stir in cooked noodles and stir fry briskly for 1-2 mins. until noodles are hot and just coated with oil. Drain with a slotted spoon and put onto a serving dish and keep warm. Heat remaining oil in the pan, add onion and stir fry for 1-2 mins. until just softened. Stir in meat and cook for a further minute, then add cucumber sticks and stir fry veg. and continue to cook for 2-3 mins. until everything is heated through. Stir sauce, pour over mixture in pan and continue to stir fry for 1-2 mins. until sauce thickens and coats the vegetables. Pour mixture over the warm noodles and serve at once.

If you prefer you can use raw pork or chicken, cut up finely and fried until cooked, and you can substitute any suitable vegetables, fresh or cooked, instead of the can of Chinese stir fry veg. — broccoli or cauliflower sprigs, 1 or 2 tomatoes cut in chunks, a few sliced mushrooms, 1 or 2 carrots peeled and finely sliced, but you won't get quite such a 'Chinesey' flavour.

TIM'S CREAM OF TURKEY OR CHICKEN SOUP
Serves 4, 6, 8

My eldest son's favourite leftover meal. Make this soup after Christmas, when you've used up most of the turkey remnants in the final sandwiches, or dump the carcass and any extra stuffing into a freezer bag and freeze to use later when you can face the thought of turkey again. I sometimes freeze the carcass when we've had roast chicken and eventually make a larger quantity of soup using the remains of several Sunday dinners.

This recipe will serve as many people as you wish, according to the size of the turkey! Allow ½-¾ pt/300-450ml finished soup per person for a really generous serving. A food processor/liquidiser is useful if you like thick soups.

Preparation and cooking time: 2-3 hours

Turkey and/or chicken carcass
Any extra stuffing
2-3 onions
1-2 chicken or veg. stock cubes and/or any extra gravy
1-2 tsp fresh snipped or dried mixed herbs
Salt, pepper
1-2 wine glasses sherry, wine or cider (or any boozy remnants you have to hand!)
To serve: **Cream, sour cream, crème fraiche or plain yoghurt**
            Handful of fresh snipped parsley or chives
            Croûtons

Put turkey and chicken carcasses and spare stuffing into your largest saucepan or casserole pot — you may have to break them up to fit the bones into the pan. Frozen carcasses can be used straight from the freezer, but allow extra time for them to defrost during the cooking process.

Peel and slice onions and put into the pan. Crumble the stock cubes over the casserole and pour in any spare gravy. Sprinkle with herbs. Cover the lot with hot water (but don't fill the pot too full or it will boil over, leave some of the bones sticking out if necessary and stir them down later). Bring soup to the boil, then reduce heat and leave to simmer with the lid on for 1½-2 hours, stirring occasionally and adding more water if needed.

When most of the meat has fallen off the bones, remove

pan from heat and strain carefully through a large sieve or fine colander into a large mixing bowl or big saucepan — take care as it's hot and splashy, so cool slightly before straining. But it's not wise to leave warm soup standing around in a warm kitchen for very long; it's better to finish it and serve at once or store in fridge or freezer until ready to reheat before serving.

My family like a really thick, creamy soup, so the next step is rather tedious. Strip the meat from the bones and place in a processor or liquidiser, add a little of the sieved liquid and purée the meat. Pour purée into the strained soup; you may have to do this several times before all the meat is used up. This cream soup is now ready to serve, or it can be frozen in plastic containers of a size suitable for your family. If you like thin soups, see below.*

To serve: heat soup over a moderate heat, then simmer for a few minutes to reheat thoroughly — it must be really hot not just warmed. Season to taste with salt and pepper, and stir in the booze if used. Pour into a large, hot tureen or individual bowls, add a swirl of cream or yoghurt and sprinkle with the snipped herbs. Add a spoonful of croûtons to each individual helping or serve them separately at the table.

To be thoroughly economical and ecological I throw the remains of the poultry carcasses onto the lawn for the birds or the hedgehog, but be careful about doing this if you have a dog, as these bones are not good for them. It's amazing how everything disappears overnight, bones and all — my proxy daughter Louise insists we have a tramp who lives at the end of the garden, but I've never seen him!

*If you prefer a thin soup to a cream one, strain the soup into the large mixing bowl or saucepan as above, adding pieces of the cooked meat and/or any leftover cooked vegetables (peas, carrots, sweetcorn, etc.), if you like. Season to taste with salt, black pepper and herbs, reheat thoroughly and serve, or cool, pour into plastic containers and freeze for future use.

RISOTTO   *Serves 4 or more*

One of our family's traditional Christmas meals, and my
youngest son's Ki's favourite. I always make far too much,
adding all the optional extras and all the tiny portions of veg. left
in the fridge, so that we end up eating 'all the good bits' and the
extra rice goes to thicken a soup or the birds get a good
Christmas meal. Traditional Italian risotto is mostly rice, cooked
in a good stock with a little onion and Italian cheese. This is an
English version to satisfy those who like some meat with every
meal! All the scrappy bits of poultry can be used up, along with
any bits of cold ham, one or two hard boiled eggs, whatever veg.
you have in the fridge, and plenty of grated cheese.

Preparation and cooking time: 40-45 mins. — Patna rice
50-55 mins. — brown rice

**12-16 oz/375-500g/4 very full cups dry, uncooked rice, Patna
(long grain) or brown**
2 large onions
2-3 cloves garlic
2 tblsp vegetable oil or turkey dripping, for frying
**2 chicken stock cubes and 1½ pt/850ml boiling water or
1½ pt/850ml turkey or chicken stock. Leftover gravy can
be added to the stock, measured into the 1½ pt/850ml.**
8 oz/250g diced cooked turkey, chicken and/or ham

Any mix of the following vegetables:
4 oz/100g mushrooms, washed and sliced
3-4 tomatoes, washed and cut into quarters or eighths
3-4 tblsp frozen or leftover cooked peas
3-4 tblsp frozen, canned or leftover sweetcorn
3-4 tblsp frozen or leftover diced mixed vegetables
4 oz/100g mature Cheddar cheese, grated
2 hard boiled eggs, shelled and sliced

Salt, pepper, Worcester sauce
1-2 tblsp grated Parmesan cheese

Wash chosen rice in several rinses of cold water to remove starch. Peel and finely chop onion and garlic, heat oil or dripping in a deep, heavy pan and fry onion over a moderate heat for 5 mins., until softened but not browned. Add washed rice and continue to fry, stirring well, for a further 4-5 mins. Dissolve stock cubes in boiling water, or heat stock and gravy mixture, and stir approximately three-quarters of the hot liquid into the rice. Cover and leave to simmer, stirring occasionally, for 10-15 mins. (Patna rice), 20-25 mins. (brown rice), until rice is tender but still *al dente,* and the liquid is almost absorbed — add more liquid during cooking if necessary, do not let the rice boil dry.

While rice is cooking prepare chosen meat and vegetables, and stir into the cooked rice, then continue cooking for a further 5 mins., stirring gently, until risotto is heated right through. Stir in the grated Cheddar cheese, and mix in sliced egg, being careful not to break up the egg too much. Season well, tip onto a hot serving platter (I usually make it in the wok and serve it straight from there), sprinkle with grated Parmesan cheese, and serve hot with a crisp green salad and an extra bowl of grated cheese.

CHINESE CHICKEN   *Serves 3-4*

This dish can be made with raw or cooked chicken, and you can use up the little pot of rice you put in the freezer last time you served rice instead of potatoes.

Preparation and cooking time: 30 mins. (cooked chicken)
40 mins. (raw chicken)

12 oz/350g boned chicken — raw or cold roast meat
2 onions

(continued overleaf)

(Chinese Chicken continued)

2 cloves garlic or ½ tsp garlic powder
4 oz/100g mushrooms
¼ cucumber
2 eating apples
1 red or green pepper (or half of each colour)
2 oz/50g butter with 1 tblsp vegetable oil for frying
4 oz/25g/1 large cup cooked rice

Sweet and sour sauce:
1 level tblsp cornflour
1 dsp soy sauce
3 tblsp vinegar
2 tblsp sugar or honey
¼ pt/150ml chicken stock (stock cube) or gravy

Slice chicken into bite-sized chunks or strips. Peel and slice onions and garlic; wash and slice mushrooms; wash and dice cucumber; wash, core and slice apples (peel if you prefer); wash and chop or slice pepper.

Heat butter and oil in a wok or large frying pan over a moderate heat, and fry raw chicken, if used, for 4-5 mins. until golden. Remove from pan with a slotted spoon. Add a little more butter and oil to pan if needed and fry onion and garlic gently for 3-4 mins. until soft. Add mushrooms, apples, cucumber and pepper and continue stir frying for a further 5 mins. until all the veg. are softened. Add cooked chicken or roast chicken, cover pan and cook gently for a further 5 mins. until meat is cooked and the vegetables are tender but not soggy.

Make the sauce while the vegetables are cooking — put cornflour into a small pan and mix to a smooth paste with the soy sauce and vinegar. Add sugar, honey and the stock or thin gravy. Put pan over a moderate heat and bring to the boil, stirring all the time, then simmer for 2-3 mins. until sauce thickens and becomes transparent.

Stir cooked rice into chicken and veg. mixture, and stir fry for a minute until really hot. Tip mixture onto a warm serving dish or serve from the wok, pour hot sweet and sour sauce over the top and sprinkle with washed finely snipped parsley if liked.

Serve with ribbon noodles or tagliatelle.

SPANISH TURKEY OR CHICKEN   *Serves 2-3-4*

An easy dish to serve after all the Christmas cooking, when you don't want to spend yet another day in the kitchen but you still have a houseful of people looking forward to a nice meal. Make in large or small quantities to suit the numbers of diners.

Preparation and cooking time: 20-35 mins. according to type of rice used, or even quicker if you use up pre-cooked rice and serve the dish cold.

For each helping allow:

2-3 oz/50-75g dry Patna or brown rice or
  4-6 oz/100-150g/1 cup cooked rice
Pinch saffron (optional)
3-4 oz/75-100g cooked turkey or chicken
1-2 spring onions or ½ small onion
1-2 tblsp canned sweetcorn
1-2 tsp vinaigrette dressing
1 tblsp mayonnaise
Few black or green olives
1-2 tsp flaked almonds or pine kernels
Salt, black pepper, cayenne or paprika pepper

Rinse raw rice thoroughly in several pans of cold water to get rid of the starch, then cook rice in a pan of boiling water with the saffron if used, for 10-12 mins. Patna rice or 20-25 mins. brown rice (or as directed on the packet), until rice is cooked *al dente*, not mushy.

While rice is cooking 'pick' turkey or chicken and slice meat into strips. Wash and slice spring onions or finely chop onion. Drain sweetcorn.

Drain rice well, tip onto a bowl and mix vinaigrette dressing with the hot rice (or with the cold pre-cooked rice). Mix meat, onion and corn into the rice, stir in mayonnaise and season to taste. Pile rice mixture onto a serving dish, garnish with olives and sprinkle with sliced almonds or pine kernels.

Serve with French bread and butter or as part of a buffet with other salads.

BOXING DAY SALAD   *Serves 2-4*

This amount serves two as a lunch or supper dish or more as one of several salads at a post Christmas buffet.

Preparation and cooking time: 15 mins.,
plus 30 mins. chilling time

3-4 cooked boiled potatoes
8 oz/225g cooked turkey or chicken
1 hard boiled egg, shelled and sliced
2 sticks celery
3-4 spring onions or ½ small onion
2 red or green eating apples with 1 tsp lemon juice
Small bunch grapes — black, green or seedless
Few green or black olives
4 tblsp mayonnaise — homemade or bought

Garnish: **lettuce leaves, parsley sprigs, paprika pepper**

Cut potatoes into bite-sized dice and put into a bowl. Cut meat into dice or strips. Trim and wash celery, chop into ½"/1cm lengths; trim, wash and chop spring onions or peel onion and chop very finely. Wash and core apples, cut into slices and toss in lemon juice. Wash grapes, halve and de-pip large grapes, leave seedless ones whole. Stone olives. Wash lettuce leaves and arrange on a serving dish. Reserve a few apple slices, grapes and olives for decoration, put rest of fruit, celery, onion, meat and egg in the bowl with the potatoes and toss gently with the mayonnaise until thoroughly coated. Spoon mixture into the serving dish on top of the lettuce. Decorate with reserved fruit, sprinkle with washed, snipped parsley and a shake of paprika and chill for 30 mins. if possible, to allow the flavours to mix.

POSH CHICKEN (OR TURKEY) MOUSSE

Serves 4-6

This makes a delicious starter or a light lunch served with fresh bread rolls. All the ingredients must be well chilled beforehand so that the mousse will set, but otherwise it's really easy to make. You will need a liquidiser or processor for this recipe.

Preparation and cooking time: 20 mins.
plus chilling time — 1-2 hours

6 tblsp white wine, cider or water
1 sachet or 3 level tsp gelatine
1 × 15 oz/425g can consommé, well chilled
1 lb/500g cooked chicken or turkey — use the leftover bits
½ pt/300ml double cream
1 tblsp lemon juice
Salt, black pepper
Cucumber slices for garnish

Heat wine, cider or water until nearly but not quite boiling, pour it into a cup, sprinkle gelatine on top and stir until dissolved. Pour consommé into a bowl and stir in the dissolved gelatine. Put into the fridge.

Liquidise or process meat. Whip cream until stiff. Mix meat into the cold consommé mixture and fold in whipped cream. Season to taste with lemon juice, salt and pepper. Spoon mousse into a 7"/18cm soufflé dish or greased spring clip cake tin and leave to set in fridge. Serve mousse either from the soufflé dish, or carefully release spring clip and turn mousse onto a cold serving plate. Decorate with cucumber slices and serve.

CHICKEN & HAM GOUGÈRE   *Serves 2-3*

A tasty way of using the 'pickings' from the poultry carcass, which can be mixed with chopped ham, mushrooms and cheese, according to availability.

Preparation and cooking time: 60-65 mins.

Filling:
1 oz/25g 1 heaped tblsp cornflour or flour
½ pt/300ml milk
1 oz/25g butter or margarine
6 oz/150g cooked chicken, turkey or ham, diced
2-4 oz/50-100g mushrooms, sliced
2-3 tblsp canned sweetcorn (optional)
2-4 oz/50-100g grated Cheddar cheese
Salt, black pepper, ¼ tsp mustard

Choux pastry:
2½ oz/65g plain flour with a pinch salt
2 eggs
2 oz/50g butter or hard type margarine
¼ pt/150ml water

Topping:
1-2 tblsp grated Cheddar or Parmesan cheese

Heat oven to 210°C/425°F/gas 6-7.

Well grease an 8″/20cm flan dish.

Make filling — put cornflour or flour into a basin and mix to a runny paste with a little of the milk. Boil remaining milk, stir it into the flour mixture, pour mixture back into saucepan, return to heat and bring back to the boil, stirring until sauce thickens. Beat in butter or marg., stir in chosen fillings and season to taste with salt, pepper, mustard and fresh snipped herbs. Put aside.

Make choux pastry — sieve flour and salt into a basin, beat eggs well in a separate basin. Put butter or margarine and water into a pan over a moderate heat and melt fat, gradually bringing to the boil. Remove pan from heat and immediately add sieved flour all at once, beating hard with a wooden spoon to form a smooth lump. Beat in egg a little at a time and beat finished mixture well. Pipe or spoon choux mixture decoratively round sides and thinly over base of greased dish, making a 'wall' of little meringue-shaped choux round the edge.

Carefully pour prepared filling into the flan case, sprinkle with grated Cheddar or Parmesan and bake in the hot oven for 20-25 mins., then reduce heat to 375°C/190°F/gas 5-6 for a further 15-20 mins. or until pastry is well risen, golden and crisp.

This is nice served with a crisp green salad, and new potatoes or bread rolls if you're hungry. For an even quicker filling use a 15 oz/450g can *condensed* cream of chicken or mushroom soup instead of white sauce.

VOL-AU-VENTS OR SUPPER PUFFS

The gougère fillings can be used to fill little vol-au-vent cases for a party or larger pastry cases for a main meal with vegetables or on their own as a snack. Bake the pastry cases as instructed on the packet if using frozen cases, or cook homemade ones. Heat filling gently, fill pastry cases and reheat for a few minutes in a hot oven before serving.

CREAMED CHICKEN MORNAY *Serves 2*

A delicious lunch or supper dish.

Prepare sauce as on page 51 for the gougère, and spoon the hot sauce into 2 individual shallow oven-proof dishes (it looks better served this way, but you can put it into one larger dish if necessary). Sprinkle tops with 2-3 tblsp fresh granary or white breadcrumbs, mixed with 1-2 tblsp Cheddar or Parmesan cheese if liked, dot with a little butter and bake in a hot oven, 200°C/400°F/gas 6-7 for 10-15 mins. until top is golden brown.

For a different topping add 1-2 tblsp chopped mixed nuts or pine kernels with the breadcrumbs.

Serve with bread rolls, garlic bread or salad.

HAM AND EGG PIE *Serves 3-4*

A useful 'fridge' meal to save a trip to the shops, and it makes a little meat go a long way. You can use bacon instead of ham if you wish.

Preparation and cooking time: 50 mins. (ham and egg)
60 mins. (bacon and egg)

8 oz/225g shortcrust pastry — bought or homemade
4 oz/100g ham or 3-4 rashers bacon
2-3 tomatoes, sliced and/or 3-4 oz/75-100g mushrooms
3-4 eggs — I allow one for each person
1 tsp mixed herbs
Salt, pepper
Milk for brushing

Heat oven to 200°C/400°F/gas 6-7.

Roll out two-thirds of the pastry and line a 7-8″/18-20cm sandwich or flan tin. Cut excess fat and rind off ham or bacon, cut into large pieces and spread over pastry base. Cover with sliced tomatoes and/or mushrooms (wash and slice large ones, wash button mushrooms and leave whole). Break eggs one at a time into a cup and slide into the pie, or beat them together and pour over the pie filling. Season with herbs, salt and pepper. Roll out remaining pastry and cover pie with pastry lid, pinching edges together well. Roll out remaining scraps of pastry, cut into leaves and decorate top of pie.

Brush pastry with milk and bake pie in the hot oven for 10-15 mins. until pastry is lightly coloured, then reduce heat to 180°C/350°F/gas 4-5 for a further 15-20 mins. (ham) or 25-30 mins. (raw bacon rashers).

Serve hot with vegetables or cold with salad, or put a slice in a lunch box as part of a packed meal. Large pies, made with the scrappy pieces of streaky bacon rashers which are often sold very cheaply, make a most economical party buffet dish, served with French bread and big bowls of crisp salads.

3 MAINLY VEGETABLES

Vegetables seem to be the most usual leftovers, just two or three potatoes, a spoonful of cabbage and a few slices of carrot. Why they weren't eaten remains a mystery, but just think of the waste over a year if you throw that amount in the bin several times a week.

Store cooked vegetables in a covered container in the fridge, and don't keep longer than a day or two before using them. A handful of cooked veg. can be eked out to go a long way — liquidised with gravy or stock for soups; used for filling omelettes, pancakes and flans; made into "vege" pasties or mixed with cooked chopped or sliced meat, ham or poultry in pies or pasties; or covered with a tasty sauce and made into a "vege gratin" for supper or as an accompaniment to meat or fish; or made into a curry with meat or hard boiled eggs — everyone has their own favourites.

Vegetable soups are fantastically economical meals, doubly so if made from leftover cooked veg. — you can experiment with all kinds of mixtures and flavours. You can, of course, buy ingredients specially to make a wide variety of soups or to mix with leftover ingredients. If you have a processor or liquidiser which saves time sieving, you can quickly produce some very tasty, filling soups, either as a starter or for a main course, using up those odds and ends of fresh veg. which are left at the back of the vegetable rack or the tiny portions of cooked veg. left over from last night's dinner. Soups are a good way of getting rid of a glut of garden produce (i.e. tomatoes or lettuce), which always seems to be ready together, especially when all your neighbours seem to have excess at the same time.

Soups made from cooked leftovers have the added advantage that they don't take nearly as long to cook as fresh ingredients, and once cooked they can be poured into plastic containers (in individual or family-sized portions) and frozen, to be quickly defrosted and reheated if not required immediately.

Soups can be as substantial as you like. Adding lentils, pre-soaked beans, pasta or dumplings (which can cook in the soup liquid with the vegetables) will make a complete meal; or top the cooked soup with thick rounds of French bread, sprinkle with grated cheese and toast under a hot grill just before serving — delicious with onion or vegetable soups. A handful of croûtons, a swirl of cream or plain yoghurt and a sprinkle of fresh snipped herbs will change a leftover dish into a special occasion.

Potatoes are often left over — there's always someone not feeling very hungry or deciding to start slimming when you've cooked a big panful. But they can be mixed with other cooked vegetables (hurrah for bubble and squeak!), sautéed on their own or with sliced onion, used as a base for creamy Spanish tortilla (one of my favourites), sliced in mayonnaise for a potato salad, puréed in soups to make them nice and thick, or mixed with other veg., cheese, meat or hard boiled eggs in pies and flans; while mashed potato can be made into plain potato fries or mixed with chopped veg., meat or fish to make savoury cakes, mixed with egg or milk and shaped into a savoury flan or topping, or heaped into potato castles as an accompaniment for tomorrow's dinner. Very small amounts of mashed potato can be shaped into one potato castle and frozen individually — eventually you'll have enough castles for a family dinner, or instant potato to pop into the oven with a meal for one.

P.S. I'm counting tomatoes as vegetables. I know they're really fruits, but they fit in better with the savouries.

Recipes using raw aubergines

Greek-style Stuffed Aubergines (p. 35)
Monday Moussaka (p. 34)

Recipes using beans

Cheating Chop Suey — raw/cooked green beans (p. 38)
Curry, Spicy Vegetable — raw/cooked green beans, cooked haricot/kidney beans (p. 70)
Egg Tortilla — cooked green beans (p. 89)
Salad, Rice — cooked green beans (p. 82)
Sauté of Roast & Boiled Veg. — cooked green beans (p. 76)
Savoury Flan — cooked green/kidney beans (p. 79)
Soup — Minestrone Mixture — cooked haricot/kidney beans (p. 65)
Vegetable Gougère — cooked green/kidney beans (p. 75)

Recipes using broccoli

Cauliflower Savoury — cooked (p. 74)
Cheating Chop Suey — raw/cooked (p. 38)
Curry, Spicy Vegetable — raw/cooked (p. 70)
Egg Tortilla — cooked (p. 89)
Monday Special — cooked (p. 67)
Sauté of Roast & Boiled Veg. — cooked (p. 76)
Savoury Flan — cooked (p. 79)
Vegetable Gougère — cooked (p. 75)

Recipes using cooked Brussels sprouts

Monday Special (p. 67)   Sauté of Roast & Boiled Veg.
                                (p. 76)

Recipes using cabbage

Bubble & Squeak — cooked (p. 75)
Coleslaw — raw (p. 95)
Soup — Minestrone Mixture — raw (p. 65)

Recipes using carrots

Cheating Chop Suey — raw/cooked (p. 38)
Coleslaw — raw (p. 95)
Curry, Spicy Vegetable — raw/cooked (p. 70)
Mixed Cheese Soufflé — cooked (p. 105)
Monday Special — cooked (p. 67)
Sauté of Roast & Boiled Veg. — cooked (p. 76)
Savoury Flan — cooked (p. 79)
Soups — General Vegetable Soup — raw/cooked (p. 62)
          (Cheating Mulligatawnyish Soup —p. 66
          Minestrone Mixture — p. 65
          Thick Vegetable & Lentil Soup — p. 65)
          Smooth Tomato Soup — raw (p. 68)
Vegetable Crumble — cooked (p. 72)
Vegetable Gougère — cooked (p. 75)

Recipes using cooked cauliflower

Cauliflower Savoury (p. 74)   Cheating Chop Suey (p. 38)
Curry, Spicy Vegetable   Egg Tortilla (p. 89)
  (p. 70) — raw/cooked   Mixed Cheese Soufflé (p. 105)
Monday Special (p. 67)   Sauté of Roast & Boiled Veg.
Savoury Flan (p. 79)   (p. 76)
Soups — General Vegetable Soup (p. 62) — raw/cooked
          (Cheating Mulligatawnyish Soup — p. 66
          Minestrone Mixture — p. 65
          Thick Vegetable & Lentil Soup — p. 65)
Vegetable Crumble (p. 72)   Vegetable Gougère (p. 75)

Recipes using raw celery

Coleslaw (p. 95)

Curry, Spicy Vegetable
(p. 70) — raw/cooked

Monday Special (p. 67)
— cooked

Cream Cheese Loaf
(p. 104)

Mixed Cheese Soufflé
(p. 105)

Salad, Boxing Day
(p. 48)

Savoury Flan (p. 79) — cooked

Soups — General Vegetable Soup (p. 62) — raw/cooked
(Cheating Mulligatawnyish Soup — p. 66
Minestrone Mixture — p. 65
Thick Vegetable & Lentil soup — p. 65)
Smooth Tomato Soup — p. 68

Tuna Continental (p. 14)   Vegetable Gougère (p. 75)
— cooked

Recipes using cooked courgettes

Cheating Chop Suey (p. 38)
— raw/cooked

Monday Special (p. 67)

Mixed Cheese Soufflé
(p. 105)

Sauté of Roast & Boiled Veg.
(p. 76)

Soups — General Vegetable Soup (p. 62) — raw/cooked
(Cheating Mulligatawnyish Soup — p. 66
Minestrone Mixture — p. 65
Thick Vegetable & Lentil Soup — p. 65)

Recipes using cucumber

Charlbury Chow Mein
(p. 40)

Coleslaw (p. 95)

Chinese Chicken
(p. 45)

Salad, Rice (p. 82)

Recipes using leeks

Soups — General Vegetable Soup (p. 62)
(Cheating Mulligatawnyish Soup — p. 66
Minestrone Mixture — p. 65
Thick Vegetable & Lentil Soup — p. 65)

Recipe using lentils
Thick Vegetable & Lentil Soup — p. 65

Recipe using lettuce
Lettuce Soup — p. 69

Recipes using marrow
Harvest Festival Special (p. 23) — raw
Soups — General Vegetable Soup (p. 62) — raw/cooked
          (Cheating Mulligatawnyish Soup — p. 66
          Minestrone Mixture — p. 65
          Thick Vegetable & Lentil Soup — p. 65)

Recipes using raw mushrooms (see also p. 123)
Cheating Chop Suey (p. 38) — raw/cooked

Chinese Chicken (p. 45)

Creamed Chicken Mornay (p. 52)

Ham & Egg Pie (p. 52)

Hubble Bubble (p. 76)

Nutty Mushroom Pasta (p. 85)

Salad, Rice (p. 82)

Chicken & Ham Gougère (p. 50)

Chinesey Fried Rice (p. 83)

Curry, Spicy Vegetable (p. 70) — raw/cooked

Mixed Cheese Soufflé (p. 105)

Risotto (p. 44)

Savoury Flan (p. 79)

Soups — General Vegetable Soup (p. 62) — raw/cooked
          (Cheating Mulligatawnyish Soup — p. 66
          Minestrone Mixture — p. 65
          Thick Vegetable & Lentil Soup — p. 65)

Tuna Continental (p. 14)   Vegetable Gougère (p. 75)

Recipes using onions
It is easy to use up leftover onion since an onion is a staple ingredient of many recipes. Therefore I list here only those recipes which use 2 onions or more.

Chinese Chicken (p. 45)
Curry, Spicy Vegetable
  (p. 70)
Risotto (p. 44)
Soups — General Vegetable Soup (p. 62)
              (Cheating Mulligatawnyish Soup — p. 66
              Minestrone Mixture — p. 65
              Thick Vegetable & Lentil Soup — p. 65)
              Tim's Cream of Turkey or Chicken Soup — p. 41
Tomato Chutney, Mahshar
  (p. 125)

Christmas Pie (p. 37)
Nutty Mushroom Pasta
  (p. 85)

Tomato Sauce, Italian (p. 126)
Vegetable Crumble (p. 72)

Recipes using parsnips

Sauté of Roast & Boiled Veg. — p. 76 (cooked)
Soups — General Vegetable Soup (p. 62) — raw/cooked
              (Cheating Mulligatawnyish Soup — p. 66
              Minestrone Mixture — p. 65
              Thick Vegetable & Lentil Soup — p. 65)

Recipes using peas

Chinesey Fried Rice (p. 83)
  — frozen
Egg Tortilla (p. 89)
  — cooked
Risotto (p. 44) —
  frozen/cooked
Sauté of Roast &
  Boiled Veg.
  (p. 76) — cooked

Curry, Spicy Vegetable
  (p. 70) — frozen/cooked
Monday Special (p. 67)
  — cooked
Salad, Rice (p. 82)
  — frozen/cooked
Savoury Flan (p. 79) — cooked
Vegetable Gougère (p. 75)
  — cooked

Recipes using peppers

Cheating Chop Suey (p. 38)
Coleslaw (p. 95)
Egg Tortilla (p. 89)
Salad, Pasta (p. 85)
Stuffed Peppers (p. 28)

Chinese Chicken (p. 45)
Curry, Spicy Vegetable
  (p. 70)
Salad, Rice (p. 82)
Tuna Continental (p. 14)

Recipes using cooked potato

Bubble & Squeak (p. 75) Christmas Pie (p. 37)
Crispy Shepherd's Pie Curry, Spicy Vegetable
  (p. 28)   (p. 70)
Egg Tortilla (p. 89) Meat Patacakes (p. 22)
Monday Special (p. 67) Moorland Pasties (p. 22)
Potato Pastry (p. 78) Potato Supper (p. 77)
Salad, Boxing Day (p. 48) Salad, Potato (p. 94)
Savoury Potato Nests (p. 26)
Soups — General Vegetable Soup (p. 62) — raw/cooked
          (Cheating Mulligatawnyish Soup — p. 66
          Minestrone Mixture — p. 65
          Thick Vegetable & Lentil Soup — p. 65)
          Lettuce Soup (p. 69) — raw
          Smooth Tomato Soup (p. 68) — raw/cooked

Recipes using cooked swede

Curry, Spicy Vegetable Savoury Flan
  (p. 70) — raw/cooked   (p. 79)
Soups — General Vegetable Soup (p. 62) — raw/cooked
          (Cheating Mulligatawnyish Soup — p. 66
          Minestrone Mixture — p. 65
          Thick Vegetable & Lentil Soup — p. 65)
Vegetable Crumble (p. 72) Vegetable Gougère (p. 75)

Recipes using sweetcorn

Chicken & Ham Gougère Chinesey Fried Rice (p. 83)
  (p. 50)   Creamed Chicken Mornay
Egg Tortilla (p. 89)   (p. 52)
Risotto (p. 44) Salad, Rice (p. 82)
Sauté of Roast & Boiled Veg. Savoury Flan (p. 79)
  (p. 76)   Spanish Turkey or Chicken
Vegetable Gougère (p. 75)   (p. 47)

Recipes using tomatoes (see also p. 123)

Cheating Chop Suey (p. 38)   Curry, Spicy Vegetable
Ham & Egg Pie (p. 52)   (p. 70)
Monday Moussaka (P. 34)   Risotto (p. 44)
Salad, Garlicky Tomato   Salad, Pasta (p. 85)
   (p. 90)   Salad, Rice (p. 82)
Savoury Flan (p. 79)
Soups — General Vegetable Soup (below)
              (Cheating Mulligatawnyish Soup — p. 66
              Minestrone Mixture — p. 65
              Thick Vegetable & Lentil Soup — p. 65)
              Smooth Tomato Soup (p. 68) — 1 lb (450g)
Stuffed Peppers (p. 28)
Tomato Chutney, Mahshar (p. 125) — 1 lb (450g)
Tomato Sauce, Italian (p. 126) — 1 lb (450g)

Recipes using turnips

Curry, Spicy Vegetable (p. 70)
Soups — General Vegetable Soup (below)
              (Cheating Mulligatawnyish Soup — p. 66
              Minestrone Mixture — p. 65
              Thick Vegetable & Lentil Soup — p. 65)

GENERAL VEGETABLE SOUP   *Serves 4, 6 or more*

Makes a good, filling 'lunch or supper' soup, using any mixture
of fresh veg. you have to hand, adding leftover cooked veg. when
the soup is nearly cooked.

   You can make little dumplings and cook them in the
simmering soup for a really filling supper dish (see page 64); or
add lentils to make a thick veg. and lentil soup (see page 65);
or some fresh cabbage, pre-soaked or canned haricot beans, raw
pasta and grated Parmesan cheese for minestrone soup (see page
65); or mix in curry powder, tabasco, Worcester sauce and rice
for mulligatawny (see page 66).

For a truly vegetarian soup, use only vegetable stock and omit bacon or any gravies made from meat juices.

Preparation and cooking time: 1¼-1½ hours

2-3 onions
1-2 cloves garlic or ¼-½ tsp garlic paste or powder

Choose a selection of veg. — you don't need everything!
1-2 leeks
2 large carrots
1 large potato
3-4 stalks celery
1 small turnip or half a small swede
1 small parsnip
Few sprigs cauliflower
1-2 courgettes or piece of marrow
2-4 tomatoes (use up the squashy ones)
Handful of mushrooms
Any cooked leftover veg. — peas, carrot, courgette,
  sweetcorn, etc.

2-3 rashers bacon (optional, not for vegetarians please!)
2 tblsp vegetable oil for frying
1 can tomatoes (optional, use a little less stock)
2 pints/1¼ litres approx. veg. or meat stock — homemade or
  use 2-3 stock cubes, adding leftover gravy to the liquid
1-2 tsp mixed herbs, fresh or dried
Salt, pepper, dash tabasco sauce
Handful fresh parsley and/or chives

Peel and wash chosen fresh veg. and slice or cut into ½"/1cm dice according to type. Peel marrow but leave skin on courgettes. Cut fresh tomatoes into quarters. Rinse and slice large mushrooms, leave small ones whole. De-rind and chop bacon.

Heat oil in a large saucepan over a moderate heat, and fry

sliced onion, chopped garlic and bacon for 4-5 mins. until onion is softened but not brown, and bacon is just crisp. Add prepared chosen root veg. (leeks, carrots, potato, celery, turnip, swede and parsnip) and fry for a further 4-5 mins., turning them over gently in the hot oil. Add canned tomatoes, pour on the stock and gravy, add herbs, stir well and bring to the boil, then reduce heat and simmer with the lid on for 20-30 mins. until the veg. are soft. Add remaining fresh veg. (cauliflower sprigs, courgettes, marrow, tomatoes, mushrooms) and continue to simmer for a further 15 mins., adding the leftover cooked veg. for the last 10 mins. of cooking time.

Season well with salt, pepper and a dash of tabasco. Sprinkle with fresh snipped parsley or chives if available and serve nice and hot.

HERB DUMPLINGS   *Serves 4 or more*

4 oz/100g self raising flour
¼ tsp salt
Really good shake of black pepper
1 tsp mixed dried or chopped fresh herbs
1-2 tsp fresh snipped parsley and/or chives
2 oz/50g shredded suet (use vegetarian suet if cooking for
    a vegetarian)
Cold water to mix

Mix all the dry ingredients thoroughly in a bowl, and stir in enough cold water to make a soft but not sticky dough. Shape into 8-10 small dumplings (they will swell while cooking), and drop them carefully into the soup for the last 20-25 mins. of cooking time, raising the heat if necessary so that the soup simmers gently to cook the dumplings.

THICK VEGETABLE & LENTIL SOUP

Serves 4, 6 or more

Lentils are very useful when making soups, as they will cook without pre-soaking and will make a thick heartening soup for a cold day. Brown and green lentils take longer to cook than red lentils.

Make up the General Vegetable Soup (as on p. 62) and when the soup is simmering add **4 oz/100g well washed and drained lentils,** allowing 40 minutes simmering time for brown or green lentils and 25 minutes for red lentils.

Serve soup with thick chunks of new granary bread and fresh creamy butter.

MINESTRONE MIXTURE

Serves 4, 6 or more

Vegetable soup with a hint of Italian influence.

General Vegetable Soup — see recipe, page 62

1 cup/6 oz/150g cooked or canned haricot or kidney beans or any other spare cooked beans which are left over. (You can use ½ cup/3 oz/75g dried beans, but this must be pre-soaked, then boiled for 5-10 mins. according to type and then cooked before adding to the veg. soup. Recommended cooking instructions for different types of dried beans will be given on the packet label, but it seems rather a fuss to cook a few beans just for a soup!)
1-2 tblsp tomato purée or ketchup
14 oz/460g can tomatoes
A thick slice of fresh hard cabbage, white or green
2 oz/50g dry uncooked vermicelli or tiny pasta shapes*
Dash of tabasco (optional)
2-3 oz/50-75g grated Parmesan cheese

Prepare the General Vegetable Soup according to recipe on page 62, stirring the cooked beans, tomato purée or ketchup and canned tomatoes into the soup with the stock — if using canned beans add the liquid from the can as well. You can use smaller amounts of vegetables in the soup, as the extra ingredients will pad it out considerably. Bring soup to the boil, reduce heat and simmer as before for about 30 minutes.

Wash and finely shred cabbage, and add to the simmering soup with the vermicelli or pasta shapes and any remaining veg. Continue to simmer for a further 15-20 mins. until veg. and pasta are tender. Season with plenty of salt and pepper and a dash of tabasco if liked, and serve topped generously with grated Parmesan cheese.

*If (like me) you always seem to cook too much pasta, and you have about a cup of cooked pasta shapes or a dollop of cooked spaghetti in the fridge, you can add this to the soup instead of cooking dry pasta. Separate the pieces with a fork (or chop spaghetti into short lengths) and add to the simmering soup for the final 10 mins. of cooking time.

CHEATING MULLIGATAWNYISH
SOUP   *Serves 4, 6 or more*

This may not please the pukka memsahib, but it's very tasty!

If you have about a cup of cooked rice left or stored in the freezer, use this; otherwise cook **2 oz/50g rice** in boiling water for 10-12 mins. white rice, 20-25 mins. brown rice. Drain and put aside.

Prepare General Vegetable Soup, see page 62. When soup is cooked, cool slightly, then liquidise, process or mash to produce a roughish purée. Return soup to saucepan and stir in —

the cup of cooked rice
1-2 tsp curry powder or curry paste
1-2 tsp Worcester sauce

Dash of soy sauce and/or tabasco
Shake of cayenne pepper

Adjust seasoning to taste. Reheat soup over a moderate heat, adding a little more water or stock if the purée seems too thick. Season with salt and pepper if required, and serve hot, sprinkled with a little fresh snipped parsley.

MONDAY SPECIAL   *Serves 1 or 2*

A quickly made lunchtime snack or light supper, made from yesterday's leftover Sunday lunch vegetables. You need a processor or liquidiser for this recipe.

Preparation and cooking time: 10 mins.

1-2 cups cooked veg. — cauliflower (my favourite), carrots, celery, boiled potatoes (thickens the soup too), peas, sprouts (rather a strong flavour), broccoli, courgettes etc., either all the same or any mixture which appeals to you
1-2 cups leftover gravy and/or stock (use a cube) — beef, chicken or veg. as preferred
½ glass sherry, red or white wine (optional but cheerful)
Juice of 1 orange or ½ cup orange juice (optional, good with carrot or courgette soup) — add to amount of stock
Salt, pepper, snipped fresh or mixed dried herbs
Dash Worcester or soy sauce, splash of tomato ketchup or a few drops of tabasco
To serve: **1-2 tsp grated Parmesan cheese**
      1-2 tsp double cream, crème fraiche or yoghurt

Purée chosen veg. in a processor or liquidiser with 1 cup gravy or stock. Put the smooth liquid into a saucepan and heat, gradually stirring in enough of the remaining gravy or stock with sherry, wine or orange juice to make a thick cream soup. Season well with salt, pepper, herbs and sauces, and serve with a swirl of cream or yoghurt and a sprinkle of cheese.

SMOOTH TOMATO SOUP   *Serves 4-6*

Super to make if you are lucky enough to have a glut of homegrown tomatoes, or it's a good way of using up that bag of squashy tomatoes left in the fridge at the weekend when the weather turned cold and no one ate much salad. You can add a can of tomatoes to make up the weight of tomatoes if necessary. You need a processor or liquidiser for this recipe.

Preparation and cooking time: about 1 hour

1-2 medium onions
1 large potato, raw or leftover cooked
1-2 carrots, raw or leftover cooked
1-2 sticks celery
1 lb/500g approx. tomatoes (and 1 can tomatoes if necessary)
2 tblsp vegetable oil for frying
1 tblsp tomato purée or tomato ketchup
1¾ pt/1 litre stock — vegetable or chicken, homemade or
    use hot water and 2 stock cubes
Bouquet garni or 1 tsp fresh snipped or mixed dried herbs
1 tsp sugar, salt, pepper
For a thicker soup: **1 tblsp cornflour, 2-3 tblsp cold milk**
To serve: **Double cream, sour cream or plain yoghurt**
        Fresh snipped parsley or chives

Peel and chop onions, peel and slice raw potato and carrot, wash and chop celery, wash and slice fresh tomatoes, slice any cooked vegetables. Heat oil in a large saucepan over a moderate heat and fry onion and celery for 3-4 mins., then add fresh or cooked potatoes and carrots and fry very gently for a further few minutes to soften but not brown all the vegetables. Add sliced fresh and tinned tomatoes (including the juice), stir in tomato purée or ketchup and add stock. Season with herbs, add sugar — it's safer to add salt and pepper later so that the soup does not get too salty.

Bring to the boil, then lower heat and simmer gently with the lid on for about 30 mins., until all the vegetables are soft and it smells delicious. Remove pan from heat, allow to cool slightly, then purée soup in a liquidiser or processor. Return soup to saucepan, season to taste with salt and pepper and reheat.

For a thicker soup: mix 1 tblsp cornflour with enough cold milk to make a smooth paste and stir into the puréed soup before reheating. Stir well while reheating, until soup thickens.

Serve with a generous spoonful of cream or yoghurt in each helping and garnish with a sprinkle of parsley or chives.

For an alternative thickening for the soup, add 1 cup cooked rice to the puréed soup before reheating, instead of thickening with cornflour. Simmer gently for a few minutes to reheat soup and rice completely. Of course, if you prefer a really thick, filling soup, thicken soup with cornflour as above, then stir in the cooked rice and heat before serving.

LETTUCE SOUP *Serves 4-6*

This is such a useful dish to make when there are too many lettuces ready in the garden and all the family wriggle their noses and twitch their ears if you suggest yet another salad for supper, that I had to include it. Serve hot or cold, and garnish with cream or yoghurt, fresh snipped chives or spring onions and a handful of croûtons. You need a liquidiser or processor for this recipe.

Preparation and cooking time: 45 mins.

1 large onion
2 large potatoes
1 lettuce (you can use the 'bolted' lettuce tops)

(continued overleaf)

(Lettuce Soup continued)

1 tblsp oil and a little butter for frying
1 or 2 stock cubes — vegetable or chicken
2 pts/1 really generous litre hot water
Salt, pepper
Garnish: **Croûtons — see page 99**
                4 tblsp double cream, sour cream or plain yoghurt
                Handful fresh parsley, chives or a few spring onions

Peel and chop onion, peel and slice potatoes, wash and shred
lettuce. Heat oil and butter in a large saucepan over a moderate
heat and fry onion for 4-5 mins. until softened. Stir in potato and
lettuce and stir fry for a few minutes. Dissolve stock cubes in
the hot water, pour over vegetables and bring to the boil. Reduce
heat and simmer with the lid on for about 20 mins. until soft.
Cool slightly, then liquidise or process to make a thick, smooth
soup. Season to taste with salt and pepper, and serve hot or cold.

To serve hot: Make croûtons, pour hot soup into a warm
tureen or individual bowls, top with a swirl of cream or yoghurt
and sprinkle with snipped parsley, chives or spring onions. The
croûtons can be floated on the top or served separately.

To serve cold: Chill soup in the fridge or freezer and serve as
above, garnished with cream or yoghurt and herbs, but omit the
croûtons, as they can make the soup greasy when cold.

SPICY VEGETABLE CURRY   *Serves 4*

Make a lovely spicy (not burning) curry, mixing the spices to suit
your taste, or play safe and use a commercial curry powder, mild
or hot as you prefer.

Preparation and cooking time: 45 mins.

2 large onions
2-4 cloves garlic or ½-1 tsp garlic powder

1-2 medium cooking or eating apples
1 tsp lemon juice
1 tblsp oil for frying
Choice of spices: ½ tsp coriander
                     ½-1 tsp cumin
                     ½-1 tsp tumeric
                     ¼ tsp cardamom
                     ¼-½ tsp cinnamon
                     large pinch grated nutmeg
                     ½-1 tsp curry paste
or 2-4 tsp curry powder, mild or hot, to taste
1 vegetable stock cube dissolved in ½ pt/300ml boiling water
2 or 3 tomatoes, quartered
1-2 tsp sugar, brown or white
1 tblsp pickle or chutney
1 tblsp sultanas
1 lb/500g mixed vegetables — carrots, cauliflower, broccoli,
   celery, cooked kidney or haricot beans, green beans, peas,
   peppers, potato, swede, mushrooms, turnip, etc., or any
   other veg. you have. Keep raw and cooked veg. separate
   at this stage.

Make curry sauce: peel and chop onions and garlic, peel and
chop apples and toss in lemon juice. Heat oil in a heavy pan over
a moderate heat and fry onion and garlic gently for 4-5 mins.,
stirring occasionally. Add chopped apple, stir in chosen
spices or curry powder and continue to fry gently for a further
2-3 mins. Dissolve stock cube in boiling water and pour it into
the mixture. Add quartered tomatoes, sugar, pickle or chutney
and sultanas, bring gradually to the boil, then reduce heat and
simmer with the lid on, stirring occasionally, for 15-20 mins.,
to make a thick sauce.

Prepare fresh vegetables, if used: cut into large bite-sized
pieces and cook in boiling salted water for 3-10 mins. (according
to kind) until tender but not mushy. Drain well, (all the different
kinds can be cooked in the same pan). Slice the cooked leftover

veg. into bite-sized chunks. Frozen peas, beans, sweetcorn, etc. can be cooked from frozen in the curry sauce. Gently stir all the veg. into the hot sauce, and simmer for a further 5-10 mins. until all the veg. are heated right through.

Serve on a bed of rice with poppadums, nan, chappati or pitta bread and side dishes.

EGG CURRY: prepare curry sauce as above, adding some vegetables to the sauce if you wish. Hard boil 1 or 2 eggs per person (simmer in boiling salted water for 10 mins., cool in cold water and peel off shells). Cook and drain rice (allow 2-3 oz/50-75g per person) and form it into a hollow ring on a serving dish. Slice eggs in half and arrange in the ring. Cover with hot curry sauce and serve with side dishes.

Poppadums: now widely available at supermarkets, both plain and spicy. Fry in a little hot oil as directed on the packet, drain well and serve hot or cold. Poppadums can also be cooked very fast in the microwave, without fat too! Place one or two at a time on a piece of kitchen paper and cook on high power for a few seconds, and you can watch the flat disks rise and become puffed and crispy.

Side dishes: salted nuts; chopped green, red or yellow peppers; chopped tomatoes; sliced banana; chopped apple (dip these in lemon juice to stop browning); chopped cucumber; finely sliced onion; chopped hard boiled egg; washed sultanas; desiccated coconut; plain yoghurt, served on its own (it's lovely and cool with the hot curry) or mixed with a little lemon juice and finely chopped cucumber; mango chutney.

VEGETABLE CRUMBLE   *Serves 2*

Use up cooked veg. in this dish, it makes a little bit go much farther!

Preparation and cooking time: 45 mins.

Topping:
4 oz/125g flour — wholemeal, white or a mixture
2 oz/50g margarine or butter
2 oz/50g grated cheese
2 oz/50g chopped mixed or cashew nuts
2 tblsp sesame and/or pumpkin seeds (optional)
Salt

Filling:
2 onions
½ lb/250g any mixture cooked veg. — cauliflower, carrots, swede, etc.
1 tblsp oil for frying
1 heaped tsp flour or cornflour
¼ pt/150ml boiling water with 1 stock cube or ¼ pt/150ml gravy
Salt, pepper
Dash tabasco or Worcester sauce, shake cayenne pepper

1-2 tomatoes thinly sliced

Heat oven to 190°C/375°F/gas 5-6.

Make topping: rub flour and fat together with fingertips until it looks like breadcrumbs (or process in mixer). Add cheese, nuts, seeds (if used), and salt. Mix well.

Make filling: peel and thinly slice onions, slice cooked veg. thickly. Put oil into a pan over a moderate heat, and fry onion gently for 4-5 mins., until soft. Stir in prepared veg. and heat through. Mix flour or cornflour with a tblsp cold water to make a runny paste. Crumble in stock cube (if used), then stir in boiling water, or stir in heated gravy. Stir the sauce into vegetable mixture and cook over a low heat for 2-3 mins. until sauce thickens. Season to taste.

Pour vegetable mixture into a 2 pt/1¼ litre deep pie dish, top with crumble mixture and smooth over with a fork. Decorate with sliced tomatoes and bake in the hot oven for 15-20 mins. until top is nicely browned.

CAULIFLOWER SAVOURY

Serves 2-4

Makes a light supper dish for two, or a lovely tasty vegetable accompaniment with cold meat — particularly if there's not a lot of meat left over.

Preparation and cooking time: 35-40 mins.

Enough cooked cauliflower or broccoli (augmented with extra veg. if liked) to make up to approx. 1 lb/500g, more or less according to appetite
3-4 rashers streaky bacon
1 onion
1 tblsp oil for frying
1 heaped tblsp flour or cornflour
½ pt/300ml milk
4 oz/100g grated cheese
1-2 tblsp fresh breadcrumbs
Salt, black pepper, paprika or cayenne pepper

Heat oven to 200°C/400°F/gas 6-7.
 Well grease a 2½ pt/1½ litre oven-proof dish.
 Break cauliflower or broccoli into sprigs, slice extra veg. Chop bacon, peel and slice onion and fry them together in a little oil over a moderate heat for 4-5 mins., until bacon is cooked. Mix in flour or cornflour and gradually stir in milk, cooking gently until sauce thickens. Mix in three-quarters of the cheese and season to taste.
 Put cauliflower or broccoli sprigs and extra veg. into the greased dish. Pour hot sauce over, mix remaining cheese with breadcrumbs and scatter over the top of the sauce. Bake in the hot oven for 10-15 mins. until crisp and golden brown on top.

VEGETABLE GOUGÈRE
Serves 2-3

Prepare as for Chicken and Ham Gougère, see page 50, but use 8 oz/250g cooked mixed vegetables (broccoli, cauliflower, celery, carrots, peas, green or kidney beans, swede, etc.) instead of the meat, or use some of both for a meat and vegetable version.

BUBBLE & SQUEAK
Serves 1, 2 or more

The ultimate leftover dish! Need I say more? Use sufficient veg. to satisfy numbers and appetites.

Preparation and cooking time: 5-10 mins.

Leftover cooked potato — boiled, roasted or mashed
Leftover cooked cabbage
These should be in the ratio of approx. 2 cups of potato to 1 cup of cabbage, but it doesn't really matter.

1 onion
Dripping, oil or butter for frying

My husband Bill's Version: slice potatoes (use boiled, roast or a mixture), break up cabbage, peel and finely slice onion. Heat fat (dripping from the roast meat if possible) in a frying pan over a moderate heat, add sliced onion and cook for 2-3 mins. until just softened. Add potato slices and cook for a few more minutes, turning frequently, until just beginning to crisp and brown. Add well drained cabbage, continue cooking and turning until all the veg. are hot and golden brown.

Eat at once, with lots of Worcester sauce, yesterday's roast meat, gravy and a side salad.

Pete's Version (this is how my daughter's man cooks it): put boiled or mashed potato into a large bowl, and mash fiercely with a potato masher. Add cabbage and mash all together. Heat fat in a frying pan over a moderate heat, carefully tip in the potato mixture and smooth into a large, thick pancake shape. Fry for 2-3 mins., shaking pan and loosening pancake from time to time to stop it sticking. Turn 'pancake' over with a fish slice and cook the other side. When lovely and golden on both sides tip onto a warm plate and eat with cold meat and gravy, or keep potato pancake warm while you fry several eggs, then slide these on top of the pancake and eat at once.

Sauté of Roast and Boiled Veg.: (yet another version). Use any leftover roast veg. — potatoes, parsnips, onions, etc. with leftover boiled veg. — cabbage, cauliflower, carrots, broccoli, peas, green beans, sprouts, courgettes, sweetcorn, etc., and a peeled, thinly sliced onion.

Heat a little dripping, oil or butter in a frying pan over a moderate heat, and fry onion slices for 2-3 mins. until soft. Add sliced roast veg. and stir fry until potatoes start to crisp. Stir in remaining boiled veg. assortment and continue to cook, turning frequently to cook evenly — adding any peas, beans, sweetcorn or other very small pieces at the last moment so that they don't get brown and too crispy. Tip onto a hot plate and serve at once. This makes a good, quick meal with cold meat, chops, bacon or sausages.

Quick Frying Pan Supper: an extension of bubble and squeak! Prepare vegetables as for bubble and squeak, either version, as above. Heat a little fat or oil in the frying pan over a moderate heat and add one or two rashers of chopped bacon per person. Fry for a few minutes, adding thinly sliced onion if liked. Stir in cooked vegetables and fry until almost cooked. Make some hollows in the vegetables and slide an egg into each, allowing one or two for each person according to appetite. Put lid on pan and fry for 1-2 mins. until eggs are cooked to your taste. Serve on warm plates and eat at once.

Hubble Bubble: yet another variation of bubble and squeak, involving vegetables and a frying pan.

Prepare veg. as for Bill's Version (page 75). De-rind and chop 1-2 rashers of bacon and wash and slice a few mushrooms. Heat dripping or oil in a frying pan over a moderate heat, and fry bacon and onion for a few minutes. Add mushrooms, potato and cabbage and continue to fry for a few more minutes until browned. Beat 1-2 eggs per person, according to appetite, and pour them over the veg. in the pan, sprinkle with a little grated Cheddar or Parmesan cheese and cook until the eggs are set — pop the pan under a hot grill for a minute to brown the top if liked. Slide onto a hot dish and eat at once.

Quick Pan Haggarty: traditionally made from raw potatoes in the North East, but this quick method makes a really substantial snack on its own or is a tasty way of serving potatoes, especially when you want to pad out the meat! Peel and slice an onion and fry it in a little dripping or oil over a moderate heat for 2-3 mins. until softened. Slice enough boiled potatoes to suit your appetite into a bowl and stir in the softened onion. Put a layer of mixed onion and potato into the frying pan, adding a little more fat if needed, scatter on a layer of grated cheese, and repeat layers until all the vegetables are used up, finishing with a good sprinkle of cheese. Fry gently, shaking pan and loosening potato with a fish slice, until the potatoes are cooked and the cheesy layers have melted — you can pop the pan under a hot grill to finish off and make a really crisp topping.

Slide onto a hot dish and eat at once. If you are only making a small amount you will get the best results using a small frying or omelette pan, to produce a crispy outside while the middle is soft with melted cheese.

POTATO SUPPER
Serves 2 as a supper,
3-4 as a vegetable

A pauper's supper dish, but a feast fit for a king when served as part of a main meal.

Preparation and cooking time: 45-50 mins.

1 lb/500g boiled potatoes
4-6 oz/150g strong Cheddar cheese
2 eggs
¼ pt/150ml/1 cup milk
Salt, pepper, nutmeg, few sprigs parsley
1 oz/25g butter
For supper dish: **1 hard boiled egg**
                        1-2 tomatoes
                        Small bunch watercress

Heat oven to 190°C/375°F/gas 5-6.

Slice cooked potatoes thinly, grate cheese. Well grease a 2½ pt/1 litre pie or shallow oven-proof dish and put in a layer of potatoes, cover with half the cheese and then put another layer using up the remaining potato. Beat eggs, stir in milk, season with salt, pepper and nutmeg and snip in parsley. Pour mixture over potatoes. Top with remaining cheese, dot with butter and cook in the hot oven for 20-25 mins., until the custard is set and the top is golden and bubbly. Serve as a posh accompaniment to meat or fish.

If serving as a supper dish on its own decorate the top with sliced tomatoes before baking, and top the cooked dish with sliced hard boiled egg and washed watercress sprigs when serving.

POTATO PASTRY   *Makes 1 lb/500g*

Use as shortcrust pastry. It makes a different crust for savoury pies, pasties and flans, and can also be used with sweet fillings. It's easier to roll out when cold, so try and allow some standing time before use.

Preparation time: 10 mins., plus 1 hour chilling time

10 oz/350g self raising flour
½ tsp salt
8 oz/250g butter or hard block margarine
6 oz/150g cold, mashed potato

Put flour and salt into a bowl, and rub in fat with fingertips until mixture resembles breadcrumbs, or process in a mixer or food processor. Add mashed potato and mix all together (if working by hand you will find this easiest with a fork). Knead into a ball. Cover bowl with cling film and leave in the fridge for about an hour.

Roll out on a lightly floured surface and use as shortcrust pastry.

If you need 8 oz/225g pastry for Quiche Lorraine (page 91), just halve the ingredients.

SAVOURY FLAN
Serves 4-6

You can put virtually any cooked meat or vegetable mixture into a flan, mixed with a creamy white or cheese sauce (I top flans with a creamy sauce and quiches with beaten eggs). Use up chicken, turkey, ham, mushrooms, cooked veg., tomatoes and hard boiled eggs as you prefer.

Preparation and cooking time: 45-55 mins.

8 oz/225g shortcrust, cheese or potato pastry (see page 110
and opposite)
Filling:
1 oz/25g/1 heaped tblsp cornflour or flour
½ pt/300ml milk
1 oz/25g butter or margarine
Salt, pepper
2-4 oz/50-100g grated Cheddar cheese (optional)
1 heaped tblsp grated Parmesan cheese (optional)
½ tsp mustard

A selection from the following ingredients as available:

4-8 oz/100-225g cooked chicken, turkey or ham, diced

4-8 oz/100-225g cooked mixed vegetables (green or kidney beans, broccoli, cauliflower, celery, carrots, peas, swede, etc.)

4-8 oz/100-225g mushrooms, sliced

4-8 oz/100-225g cooked or drained canned sweetcorn

2-4 tomatoes, sliced

1-4 hard boiled eggs, sliced

1-2 tblsp grated Cheddar or Parmesan cheese (optional)

Heat oven to 200°C/400°F/gas 6-7.

Roll out pastry, line a 7-8"/18-20cm flan dish and bake blind as for Quiche Lorraine − see page 92.

Prepare filling − put cornflour or flour into a basin and mix to a runny paste with a little of the milk. Boil remaining milk, stir it into the flour mixture, pour mixture back into saucepan, return to heat and bring back to the boil, stirring all the time until sauce thickens. Beat in butter or margarine, season with salt and pepper. Stir in cheese and mustard if used.

Arrange the chosen, prepared meat and/or vegetables in the part baked flan case and cover with the sauce. Sprinkle top with grated cheese if liked, and bake in the hot oven for 15-20 mins., until flan is hot right through and the top is golden and bubbling.

The flan is delicious served warm with jacket or new potatoes and salad.

4 RICE & PASTA

If you have a freezer you need never throw away cooked rice; it freezes well in small plastic containers or double plastic bags (to stop accidental leakage all over the freezer), ready for use in rice salads, fried rice dishes, stuffed vegetables, thickening soups, etc. — it saves a lot of bother if you have the rice already cooked for most of these dishes. Rice may be added to soups or sauces while still frozen, it will soon defrost in the hot liquid. It can be defrosted in the microwave if you're in a hurry, or left to defrost more slowly if there is time.

Cold, cooked pasta shapes can be used in a salad with vegetables, meat or fish, or mixed into a hot sauce and served hot. Cooked noodles can be fried in a little hot oil to make delicious crispy noodles. Cold spaghetti I'm not too keen on, so either chop it in small pieces and add to vegetable soup, or feed the birds with 'instant worms!'.

Recipes using cooked rice

Chinese Chicken (p. 45)

Salad, Rice (below)

Spanish Turkey or Chicken (p. 47)

Stuffed Peppers (p. 28)

Chinesey Fried Rice (p. 83)

Soup — Cheating Mulligatawnyish Soup (p. 66)

Tuna Continental (p. 14)

Recipes using cooked pasta

Charlbury Chow Mein (p. 40)

Salad, Pasta (p. 85)

Nutty Mushroom Pasta (p. 85)

Soup — Minestrone Mixture (p. 65)

RICE SALAD　　　　　　　　　*Serves 2 or more*

This is the cold version of fried rice. It can be made into a light meal with lots of extras, or left plainer as an accompaniment.

Preparation and cooking time: 15 mins.

2 cups cooked rice (you will need to cook 1 cup dry rice/4 oz/ 100g dry rice if there's none ready cooked)

4 tblsp French dressing (mix 3 tblsp oil with 1 tblsp wine vinegar or lemon juice, pinch sugar, salt, pepper)

½ small onion or 3-4 spring onions

2 oz/50g frozen mixed veg. and/or peas, cooked and drained

2 oz/50g canned sweetcorn, drained

Few sprigs fresh parsley and/or chives

Extras:

2 oz/50g mushrooms, washed and sliced

Few rings green or red peppers, chopped

1 hard boiled egg, cut in chunks

Small piece cucumber, diced
1 or 2 tomatoes, rough chopped or chunked
2 tblsp canned or pre-cooked kidney, flageolet or aduki beans, well drained
Handful black or green olives
2 oz/50g cooked, peeled prawns
2 oz/50g cooked ham, chicken, etc., diced

Put cooked rice into a serving bowl. Stir French dressing well, then pour over rice and mix all together. Peel and finely chop onion or trim and chop spring onions and stir into the rice with the cooked mixed veg. and sweetcorn. Add chosen extras and mix gently. Cover with cling film and leave in a cool place until ready to serve — this salad will benefit from standing for at least 30 mins. to absorb all the different flavours.

To serve, stir salad again and top with a little fresh snipped parsley or chives.

CHINESEY FRIED RICE

Serves 2 or more

Serve plain as an accompaniment or mixed with lots of extras to make a main meal. It's a good way of using up all the little bits left in the fridge, as the amounts used can vary according to availability.

Preparation and cooking time: 20 mins.

1 egg
½ small onion or 3-4 spring onions
1 clove garlic or ½ tsp ground garlic
2 tblsp approx., vegetable oil
2 cups cooked rice (or cook 1 cup/4 oz/100g dry rice)

(continued overleaf)

(Chinesey Fried Rice continued)

1 tblsp soy sauce
Salt, pepper
Few sprigs fresh herbs — parsley, chives, mint, tarragon, etc.

Extras:
2 oz/50g diced cooked ham, chicken or turkey
2 oz/50g cooked, peeled prawns
Few mushrooms, sliced
2 tblsp frozen peas
2 tblsp canned or frozen sweetcorn
2 tblsp canned bamboo shoots, sliced
2 tblsp cashew nuts or pine kernels

Beat egg in a small basin. Peel and finely chop onion and fresh garlic or trim, wash and chop spring onions. Prepare chosen extras (the peas and sweetcorn can be cooked from frozen, they will defrost in the pan).

Heat oil in wok or frying pan over a moderate heat, pour in beaten egg and fry until cooked. Put egg onto a plate and cut into thin strips.

Add more oil to pan and fry chopped onion and garlic for 2-3 mins. until soft. Add chosen extras and continue stir frying for about 2 or 3 minutes until cooked. Remove with a slotted spoon and put aside.

Add a little more oil if needed, tip the rice into the pan and stir fry until rice is hot and all the grains are separate. Stir in soy sauce and mix well to coat the rice. Add cooked egg and extras, and fry until everything is nice and hot. Season with salt and pepper and sprinkle with a few snipped herbs if available. Serve at once.

If serving fried rice as an accompaniment, you can omit the egg and just stir in a few vegetables to add a bit of colour to the dish.

PASTA SALAD   *1, 2 or more*

Serve as a salad accompaniment, or add cold cooked meat, sausage, salami, tuna fish or prawns to make it into a complete light meal.

Preparation time: 15 mins.

Use up any cooked pasta shapes — shells, bows, etc.
Allow approx. 1 cup/4 oz/100g cooked pasta per person (if you need to cook the pasta allow 2 oz/50g dry pasta for each serving)

For each cup of cooked pasta allow:
1 tblsp finely chopped onion
1 tomato, cut in chunks
1-2 rings green or red pepper, chopped
2 tblsp tomato- or curry-flavoured mayonnaise
1-2 oz/25-50g cooked chicken, turkey, ham, salami or sausage
1-2 tblsp drained, canned tuna fish or cooked prawns
Few green or black olives — stoned
Parsley for garnish

Put cooked pasta into a bowl, mix in chopped onion, tomato, peppers, add flavoured mayonnaise and turn mixture over gently until everything is well coated. Slice meat (if used) into bite-sized pieces or dice, and mix in to the salad, or mix in tuna or prawns if used. Turn salad into a serving dish, garnish with olives and snipped parsley, cover and leave to chill for at least 30 mins. if possible to absorb the flavours before serving.

NUTTY MUSHROOM PASTA   *Serves 4*

A good 'store cupboard' meal, using up the mushrooms, the half tub of yoghurt and that carton of cream cheese left in the fridge. Much more substantial than it may appear from the recipe —

lots of energy-giving carbohydrates for pre-regatta rowing eights!

Preparation and cooking time: 35 mins.

12 oz/300g pasta shells, bows, spirals, etc.*
1 tsp cooking oil
2 onions
1-2 cloves garlic or ¼ tsp garlic paste or powder
8 oz/225g mushrooms
1-2 tblsp oil for frying
3-4 oz/75-100g cream or curd cheese
3-4 oz/75-100g plain yoghurt, soured or double cream
4-6 tblsp roughly chopped walnuts, cashew nuts or pine kernels
Handful fresh parsley
Salt, pepper, shake of paprika pepper

Half fill a large pan with hot, salted water, add 1 tsp cooking oil
and bring to the boil. Stir in pasta and cook for 6-8 mins., until
al dente, not soggy. Drain well and keep warm.

While pasta is cooking, peel and finely chop onions and fresh
garlic. Wash and slice mushrooms. Heat oil in a pan over moderate
heat and fry onion and garlic for 4-5 mins. until soft but not brown.
Add mushrooms, cooking gently for a further 4-5 mins. until veg.
are cooked. Stir in cream or curd cheese, yoghurt, soured or
double cream, and nuts and heat gently, stirring carefully to make
a creamy sauce. Stir pasta into the creamy mixture, mixing gently
to coat pasta with the sauce and heating thoroughly. Stir in snipped
parsley and season to taste.

Pile onto a warm serving dish and garnish with a shake of
paprika and a little more parsley.

This is nice served with a crisp mixed salad and garlic bread.

*You could use up leftover cooked pasta in this dish; allow 1-2
cups cooked pasta per person. Warm the pasta in the microwave
or cook for 1-2 mins. in boiling salted water with a little oil to
reheat it before adding to the sauce.

5 EGGS

I think immediately of eggs whenever I need to produce an unexpected meal — there are usually a few eggs in the fridge, and most egg dishes don't take long to prepare and cook.

I know you don't really have eggs left over, apart from the odd yolk or white (for which there are separate recipes), after all, eggs keep fresh in the fridge or a cool larder for a couple of weeks, but they are so handy for mixing with leftovers to make up delicious lunch and supper dishes as well as puddings that I think they should have a chapter in their own right.

In view of the publicity over salmonella in eggs, take care about the eggs you buy and store them sensibly and hygienically — eggs have porous shells and should never be stored where they are in contact with uncooked meat or fish, dust or dirt of any kind. They also absorb smells through the shells, so beware if you are buying fresh fish, washing powder, household cleaners, firelighters, etc., and keep them in separate shopping bags. Heed

the advice on fresh eggs given out by the health authorities —
only buy eggs from a reputable supplier and *do not serve raw
or lightly cooked egg dishes to babies, pregnant women or the
elderly unless you're sure that the eggs are free from bacteria*
— there are egg substitutes available in the shops (although you
may have to search for them) which you may prefer for safety
reasons instead of fresh eggs. Don't panic, but do take reasonable
care with egg cookery.

Recipes using eggs

Bread & Butter Pudding
  (p. 129)
Drinking Egg or Boozy Nog
  (p. 115)
Egg Nests (p. 89)
Ham & Egg Pie (p. 52)
Magic Islands (p. 135)
Poor Knights' Pudding
  (p. 134)
Queen's Pudding (p. 132)
Quick Frying Pan Supper
  (p. 76)
Salad, Boxing Day (p. 48)
  — hard boiled
Salad, Rice (p. 82)
  — hard boiled

Bread "Pudden" (p. 129)
Curry, Egg (p. 72)
  — hard boiled
Egg Mayonnaise (p. 94)
Egg Tortilla (p. 89)
Hubble Bubble (p. 76)
Mixed Cheese Soufflé
  (p. 105)
Potato Supper (p. 77)
Quiche Lorraine (p. 91)
Risotto (p. 44)
  — hard boiled
Salad, Potato (p. 94)
  — hard boiled
Savoury Flan (p. 79)
  hard boiled

Recipes using egg yolks

Cheese Pastry (p. 110)
Mayonnaise, Gorgeous Homemade (p. 92):
        Egg Mayonnaise (p. 94)
        Coleslaw (p. 95)
        Potato Salad (p. 94)
Magic Islands (p. 135)   Poor Knights' Pudding
Tidy Up Trifle (p. 138)   (p. 134)

Recipes using egg whites

EGG NESTS   *Serves 1, 2, 3 or more*

Allow 1 or 2 eggs per person, according to appetite. Prepare potato nests as for Savoury Potato Nests, page 27, making one or two nests each, or a large nest, and bake in the hot oven for 3-4 mins. (small) or 6-7 mins. (large), until nest is hot but not brown. Remove from oven and carefully slide required number of eggs into the nests, top each egg with a dab of butter and a sprinkle of grated cheese (optional) and put nests back into the oven for a further 5-8 mins. (small) or 10-12 mins. (large) or until eggs are cooked to your liking, and the nests are crisp and golden.

Serve at once, on their own, with salad or baked beans according to taste.

EGG TORTILLA   *Serves 1 or 2*

A delicious savoury omelette, far more substantial than it appears from the recipe — in Spain they are eaten as starters but I find them more of a main meal. Tortilla is cooked flat, like a thick pancake, traditionally mixed with a little onion and potato, but you can add cooked meat and vegetables, according to availability and taste. Make tortilla in a small omelette pan to make a thick omelette, soft and creamy inside, or make double quantity in a larger pan, which can be cut into slices to serve 2 or 3 people.

Preparation and cooking time: 15-20 mins.

Extras:

Cooked meat: 2-3 tblsp diced cooked turkey, chicken, ham, salami, garlic sausage, etc.

English sausage: 1 or 2 cold cooked sausages, sliced

Bacon: 1 or 2 rashers bacon, chopped and fried with the onion

Vegetables: 1-2 tblsp cold, cooked veg. (peas, sweetcorn, green or kidney beans, sliced cauliflower, broccoli, mixed veg., etc.)

Peppers: 1 or 2 rings green or red peppers, chopped and cooked with the onion

For each omelette (7"-8"/20cm pan) allow:
½ onion
1 clove garlic
2 or 3 boiled potatoes or cooked new potatoes
2 or 3 eggs
1 tsp cold water per egg
Salt, pepper, pinch dried or fresh snipped mixed herbs
1 tblsp oil for frying (traditionally olive oil)

Prepare extras if used. Peel and chop onion and garlic, dice cooked potatoes. Put eggs, water, seasoning and herbs into a basin and beat with a fork. Heat oil in omelette pan over a moderate heat and fry onion and garlic for 4-5 mins. until soft (add bacon and peppers if used). Add diced potatoes and fry until potato is thoroughly heated, adding any other extras, but do not let the veg. get brown and crispy.

Heat the grill and warm a plate on it.

Pour beaten egg mixture into pan, covering the veg. and cook without stirring until the base is firm but the middle is soft and the top is still wet, shaking pan occasionally to stop omelette sticking. Place pan under the hot grill for a few moments, until top is just set (do not overcook) and the middle is still soft. Slide onto the warm plate and serve at once.

This is nice with a *garlicky tomato salad* — slice some firm tomatoes and arrange on a shallow dish. Sprinkle with a little finely chopped onion and garlic, dribble a spoonful of French dressing over the top and garnish with black olives and a little washed, finely snipped parsley.

French Omelettes: the 'extras' can be used to fill French omelettes. Warm chosen filling through in a small pan with a little oil, tip onto cooked omelette, fold and serve at once.

QUICHE LORRAINE   *Serves 4-6*

'Real men' will eat this, it's delicious, and uses up the odd bits left in the fridge! Make a large quiche in a flan dish or ring, or individual quiches in patty tins — these little ones are nice for a starter, as part of a buffet supper, a packed lunch or a picnic. Use up that one rasher of bacon, the scrappy bits of cheese or the pickings from chicken, turkey or a piece of ham.

Preparation and cooking time: *1¼-1½ hours (large quiche)*
55-60 mins. (small ones)
8 oz/225g shortcrust, cheese or potato pastry, (made with
8 oz/225g flour) — see p. 110 and p. 78

Filling:
1-2 onions
2-3 rashers bacon (optional)
1 tblsp vegetable oil
2-4 oz/50-100g cooked chicken, turkey or ham (optional)
2-4 oz/50-100g Cheddar cheese
2 eggs
½ pt/300ml milk, pouring cream or a mixture
Salt, black pepper, pinch mustard
1 heaped tblsp Parmesan cheese

Heat oven to 190°C/375°F/gas 5-6.

Roll out chosen pastry and line a 7-8″/17-20cm flan dish. Prick pastry all over with a fork and cover flan with a piece of cooking foil, pressed gently into the flan shape. Bake in the pre-heated oven for about 10 mins. until pastry is just set. Remove foil and return to oven for 5 mins. until still pale but crisp. Remove from oven.

Make filling: peel and finely chop onions, chop bacon (if used). Heat oil in a pan over a moderate heat and fry onion and bacon for 3-4 mins. until onion is soft and bacon nearly cooked. Spoon into flan case and cover with diced chicken, turkey or ham if used, and sprinkle with the grated Cheddar cheese.

Break eggs into a basin and beat well with a fork. Mix in milk and/or cream, season well with salt, pepper and mustard and pour mixture over filling in flan case. Sprinkle with grated Parmesan cheese.

Bake in the hot oven for 40-45 mins., until well risen and golden, reducing oven heat to 180°C/350°F/gas 4-5 after 20 mins. if the pastry is getting too brown.

Serve hot or cold.

Small Tartlets: roll out chosen pastry, cut into 4″/10cm rounds, and line 12 patty tins (no need to pre-bake these little cases). Prepare filling as above and divide between the prepared cases. Bake in the hot oven for 20-25 mins. until risen and golden. Serve hot or cold.

GORGEOUS HOMEMADE
MAYONNAISE   *1 cup/¼ pt/150ml*

An instant way of using up any number of egg yolks. Forget all the rumours about making mayonnaise – this is a really easy, authentic and delicous recipe, and it can be made using a whisk, wooden spoon or electric mixer. The plain mayonnaise is super with salads, hard boiled eggs, cold salmon, prawns, tuna, cooked meats or jacket potatoes. It makes a good base for dips, flavoured with tomato purée, lemon, garlic or curry, or can be mixed with

Stilton, strong Cheddar or avocado.

Always buy eggs from a reliable source. However, if you are still worried about salmonella do not serve fresh mayonnaise to young children, the elderly or pregnant ladies — instead buy a jar of good commercial mayonnaise for them.

Preparation time: 15 mins.

All ingredients must be at room temperature or the mixture may curdle. Take eggs from fridge at least 30 mins. before use.

For each egg yolk allow approx.:
2 tsp lemon juice or vinegar (wine or cider vinegar is best)
Large pinch salt
Small pinch dry mustard or dab made mustard
Shake pepper
¼ pt/150ml/1 cup olive oil (or any vegetable oil)

Beat yolk in a basin with 1 tsp lemon juice or vinegar, and seasonings. Gradually add oil, a drop at a time at first (drip it off a teaspoon), beating all the time. As the sauce thickens the oil can be added faster, beating hard until all the oil is mixed in. Taste and adjust seasoning, adding a little more lemon juice or vinegar if needed, and stirring in a tsp of warm water (room temperature) if it's still too thick. The mayonnaise should be thick and creamy.

If by any chance the mayonnaise curdles and won't thicken, don't despair. Separate another egg (at room temperature), beat the yolk and then beat the curdled mayonnaise, a drop at a time, into the new yolk. Gradually add any remaining oil, beating all the time, and check seasoning as before. Homemade mayonnaise will keep for a few days in a covered jar or dish in the fridge, but never keep fresh egg dishes for very long.

Some extra flavourings — mix them into the mayonnaise when adjusting the flavouring.

½-1 tsp tomato purée or tomato sauce
Good dash of tabasco
1 tsp extra lemon juice and a little finely grated lemon rind
¼ tsp garlic powder or garlic paste
¼ tsp curry powder or chilli powder with a shake of tabasco

QUICK DISHES USING MAYONNAISE

EGG MAYONNAISE

Make as a starter or a main course.

For each person allow 1 egg as a starter or 2 as a main course.

Hard boil required number of eggs (simmer for 10 mins. in salted water, cool in cold running water), peel and rinse eggs to get rid of all the bits of shell.

Arrange a bed of washed shredded lettuce on a large serving dish or individual plates, slice eggs in rings or cut in half lengthways, and arrange on the lettuce, cut-side-down if halved. Coat eggs with prepared mayonnaise and garnish with cucumber, tomatoes, green or red pepper strips, cress, watercress, etc. as available. Sprinkle a little paprika, snipped parsley or chives on top of the mayonnaise and serve with brown or granary bread or rolls and butter.

POTATO SALAD

Uses up eggs and boiled potatoes (although we like it so much I often cook potatoes in order to make it). Useful as a 'filler' as part of a barbecue buffet.

Slice boiled old or new potatoes into large bite-sized chunks, allowing 1-2 potatoes per person (more if they're tiny new ones). Mix potato pieces with mayonnaise (you will need approximately 1 tblsp mayonnaise for each person), turning the potatoes over until all the pieces are coated. Cut 1 or 2 shelled hard boiled eggs into chunks and mix them in gently, adding a handful of washed, snipped parsley, chives or spring onions. Pile salad into a serving dish and garnish with a little more snipped fresh herbs.

COLESLAW

Cabbage salad — use a base of crisp hard cabbage, white or green, or Chinese leaf lettuce, mixed with whatever fresh veg. you have to hand.

Shred, wash and drain a good slice of hard cabbage and put it into a bowl. Add 1 or 2 carrots, peeled and shredded; 1 small onion, peeled and finely chopped or 2-3 washed, chopped spring onions; a few slices red or green peppers, chopped; small slice red cabbage, washed, drained and shredded; an eating apple, cored and chopped and mixed with a little lemon juice to stop browning; 1-2 sticks celery, chopped; ¼ cucumber, chopped or cut into sticks; 1 tblsp sultanas; and a handful of coarsely chopped walnuts — use whatever you fancy. Mix salad with 2-4 tblsp prepared mayonnaise, heap into a serving dish and serve with cold meats, fish or quiche.

CHEESY LEMON BITES *Makes about 20*

A different 'nibble' to serve with pre-dinner drinks, and a useful way to use up the egg whites left over from the mayonnaise you made for the starter! It's best made from hard, dry cheese if you have some to use up, or use Parmesan on its own or a mixture. A food processor or mixer is useful for this recipe.

Preparation and cooking time: 35-40 mins.

3 oz/75g/3 heaped tblsp cheese — Cheddar, Parmesan, etc, finely grated
3 oz/75g/3 heaped tblsp ground almonds
2-3 tsp grated lemon rind
3 egg whites

Heat oven to 150°C/300°F/gas 2-3. Line a flat baking tray with silicone or oiled greaseproof paper.

Mix grated cheese, ground almonds and lemon rind. Beat egg whites until stiff with a mixer or processor, then fold into the cheese mixture using a metal spoon, being careful not to burst the air bubbles in the egg white. Put teaspoonfuls of the mixture onto the baking tray, and bake in the cool oven for 20-25 mins. until golden and crisp.

Remove from oven and cool on a wire tray. Use the same day if possible, or store in an airtight tin or plastic box, but not in the fridge as they go soft.

CHEESE MERINGUES *Each egg white makes 6-8 shells*

A change from the very sweet dessert meringues. Serve at tea time or with drinks, plain or sandwiched together with a little cream cheese, or make really tiny meringues to garnish consommé. A food processor or mixer is useful for this recipe.

Preparation and cooking time: 1½-2 hours

For each egg white use 1½ oz/40g grated cheese (use up bits of Cheddar or whatever is in the fridge), a tsp of Parmesan mixed with it gives a good 'sharp' taste
Pinch salt
Pinch mustard
Cream cheese to sandwich together
Paprika pepper to decorate

Heat oven to 100°C/200°F/gas ¼-½. Line 1 or 2 baking trays with silicone or oiled greaseproof paper, allow 8-12 shells on each tray.

Grate cheese finely, mix with Parmesan if used, salt and mustard. Whisk egg white in a large bowl using a mixer or processor, until very stiff. Use a metal spoon and fold cheese mixture into the egg, taking care not to burst the bubbles in the egg white. Use a spoon to drop meringue onto the prepared sheet, making large or small shell shapes, leaving space for meringues to spread and rise. Bake in the cool oven for 1-1½ hours according to size, until pale golden, crisp and dry.

Remove from oven and cool on a wire tray. Use at once or store in a plastic box or airtight tin.

Sandwich together just before use if liked, with a little cream cheese, garnish with a sprinkle of paprika and arrange on a serving dish, or pile unfilled meringue shells into a bowl and serve plain. Tiny shell can be floated on top of clear soup at the last minute, to make a pretty garnish at posh dinner parties.

6 BREAD & CHEESE

I'm sure everyone must occasionally have some leftover bread, especially if you have a family who are unable to resist the lovely new loaf and push yesterday's bread to the back of the bread bin 'for toast later!'. Instead of throwing all these odd crusts out for the birds, really organised people will make breadcrumbs or croûtons and store them in the freezer for later use. If you can't be bothered doing that (or know you'll never find them again in the depths of the freezer!), there are lots of recipes for savoury dishes and puds which will use up the last slices of bread. Many vegetarian dishes include breadcrumbs, especially the savoury lunch and supper dishes, so if you always seem to have bread over, why not invest in a copy of *No meat for me, please!** and try out some of the suggestions there?

---

*one of my other books also published as a *Paperfront*.

Breadcrumbs — these can be made very quickly if you have a liquidiser or processor, otherwise it's a tedious grater job! Store in double polythene bags (in case of accidents) which will tuck into a corner of the freezer and defrost quickly when needed for use in "vege" dishes, stuffings, breadsauce, sweet and savoury toppings, fruit charlotte and lots of other puds.

Croûtons — sprinkle a good handful over thick creamy soups in winter or garnish a hot summer consommé with lots of parsley and just a few croûtons. They can be cooked and frozen on a flat tray, then stored in a tub or double polythene bag ready to defrost and crisp in a hot frying pan for a few moments.

Cut the leftover bread into ½"/1cm cubes, and fry in a little vegetable oil and a knob of butter in a large frying pan over a moderate heat, turning croûtons frequently until they are crisp and golden on all sides, taking care that the fat does not get too hot or the bread will burn. Remove croûtons from pan and drain on kitchen paper. Olive oil gives a lovely flavour to the croûtons, and for a gorgeous garlic flavour rub the cold frying pan well with a crushed clove of garlic before heating the oil, but be careful this does not overpower the flavour of the more bland, creamy soups.

Toppings — Mix fresh breadcrumbs with grated cheese — Cheddar type or Parmesan — and/or a spoonful of chopped fresh or dried mixed herbs, and sprinkle over meat, fish or vegetables in a sauce, dot with butter and bake for a few minutes in a hot oven or flash under a hot grill to crisp.

For a different *crispy sweet topping*, a change from pastry or the traditional flour, butter and sugar crumble, fry fresh breadcrumbs in butter for a few minutes over a medium heat (approx. 4 oz/100g crumbs to 2 oz/50g butter). Mix in 2 oz/50g demerara or granulated sugar and the same amount of chopped mixed nuts or flaked almonds, and spoon this over prepared pie fruit in a pie dish, and bake in a moderate oven as for a fruit pie.

For a *crispy savoury topping* (makes a really savoury shepherd's pie), omit sugar and nuts from the above recipe and mix in 2 oz/50g grated mature Cheddar cheese with the fried crumbs, spread over meat, fish or vegetables in a sauce in a pie dish, and bake in a moderate oven as before.

French bread — don't throw away the leftover half of yesterday's French loaf, fill it with herb or garlic butter (see page 102), wrap in foil and freeze (overwrap in polythene to stop the garlic flavouring everything else in the freezer). Heat before serving; the bread will crisp and taste just like new.

Use slices of leftover French or garlic bread to top hot soup for a filling snack on a cold day.

Cheese is a really marvellous food, either in its own right or mixed with other ingredients, fresh or leftover, to give nourishment, flavour and texture to many savoury dishes. You can substitute one cheese for another in most recipes, according to what's in the fridge, although it's best to stick to the same kind of cheese as specified in the recipe — hard, crumbly or melting cheeses (Cheddar, Double Gloucester, Edam, Lancashire, Leicester, Gruyère, Emmental etc.), soft and cream cheeses (Brie, Camembert), or blue cheese (Stilton, Danish blue, Cambozola, Dolcellate) or any of the many similar cheeses too numerous to mention. Choose according to taste and price, but the end results will be similar to the original recipe with your own personal touch.

Odds and ends of cheese need not be thrown away, even if the outside looks a bit hard or mouldy. Just slice off the outside layer (birds and cats love it) and use up the scrappy bits in cooking, either grated over veg., in sauces or as part of a meal in its own right.

Recipes using bread

Recipes using breadcrumbs (p. 99)

Recipes using biscuits

Recipe using cake/Swiss roll

Recipes using cheese

(continued overleaf)

Recipes using cream cheese

GARLIC AND HERB BREAD   *1 French loaf*

A useful standby to have in the freezer, it makes a scratch meal seem quite luxurious, and is a good way of using up the extra loaf you didn't need after all. You can also fill and freeze bread rolls, which will defrost and bake very quickly in an emergency!

Preparation and cooking time: 15 mins. − rolls
20-25 mins. − French loaf

2 cloves garlic or ½-1 tsp garlic powder or paste
4 oz/100g butter
Handful fresh herbs − parsley, chives, etc. as available
1 long French loaf or 6-8 bread rolls
Large piece of foil for wrapping

Heat oven to 200°C/400°F/gas 6-7.

Peel and crush fresh garlic, then beat garlic into the butter until soft and creamy. Beat in washed, finely snipped herbs if used. Make sure the loaf will fit into your oven; if not, cut it in two and make two shorter parcels. Cut loaf nearly through into generous slices (be careful not to slice right through or loaf will drop to bits), or slice rolls vertically into 3 portions (again don't cut right through). Butter thickly between the slices, press loaf or rolls together again and wrap loosely in kitchen foil (wrap rolls individually).

Bake wrapped bread in the hot oven, allowing 5 mins. for rolls and 10 mins. for French bread. Unfurl and serve hot. To freeze — put foil-wrapped bread or rolls into a polythene bag (the flavour is very pungent) and freeze until needed. Defrost before baking. (If you have a microwave, remember that the loaf is wrapped in foil and unwrap to defrost, rewrapping to bake!)

HERB BREAD

If you don't like garlic, omit garlic from the above recipe and make a herb loaf, adding a really generous handful of freshly chopped or snipped mixed herbs and a tsp lemon juice to the butter.

CHEESE BREAD

A delicious variation of herb bread, using up odds and ends of cheese as well.

2 oz/50g butter
6-8 oz/150-200g Cheddar, Edam, Double Gloucester, etc.
Handful fresh herbs — parsley, chives, etc.
3-4 spring onions or 1 tsp very finely chopped onion —
   optional
1 French loaf or 6-8 rolls
Piece of cooking foil

Beat butter until soft. Finely grate cheese and beat into the butter, adding washed snipped or chopped herbs and onions, if used. Slice, fill and bake as for garlic bread.

CREAM CHEESE LOAF

Use recipe and method as for Cheese Bread, but use **6-8 oz/ 150-200g cream cheese** instead of the finely grated Cheddar. One or 2 sticks of washed, very finely chopped celery can be used instead of the onion if you prefer it.

CHEESE DIPS AND SPREADS

Feel really virtuous and use up the odds and ends of cheese that seem to accumulate in the fridge, by making them into a dip or a spread, to use at once or freeze for future use. The amounts given in the recipes are approximate — use up whatever amounts you have available.

   If making spreads to use in sandwiches omit the liquid to produce a stiffer spread.

Cheddar Cheese Dip

2 oz/50g Cheddar cheese — or any hard type cheese
1 oz/25g butter
2-3 tblsp milk, white wine or cider
Few drops Worcester or tabasco sauce
Salt, black pepper
Shake cayenne or paprika pepper

Grate cheese. Put butter into a basin and beat until soft, gradually beating in the cheese, and mix to a 'dip' consistency with milk, wine or cider (you can use up the end of the wine bottle!) Season to taste and pile into a small serving dish. Garnish with a shake of cayenne or paprika and serve with crudités, crisps, savoury biscuits or homemade cheese straws.

Blue Cheese Dip

2 oz/50g butter
4 oz/100g blue cheese — Stilton, Danish Blue, Gorgonzola, etc.
2-3 tblsp milk, wine, cider or dry sherry
Black pepper
1-2 tblsp chopped walnuts (optional)

Beat butter until soft and creamy, crumble blue cheese and beat it gradually into the butter, adding enough liquid to make a soft dip. Season with salt and pepper, stir in walnuts if used and heap into a small serving dish. Serve with crudités, cheese straws or pipe or spoon onto 2″/5cm lengths washed celery for party 'nibbles'.

Cream Cheese Dip

4 oz/100g cream cheese or Cambozola
1 oz/25g butter
Handful fresh parsley or chives
Few spring onions
1 or 2 tsp milk, wine or cider

Beat cream cheese and butter until soft. Beat in washed snipped herbs and very finely chopped spring onions, adding a few drops of liquid if the mixture is too stiff. Pile into a serving dish and serve with crudités, crisps or biscuits as before.

MIXED CHEESE SOUFFLÉ

Serves 2-4 according to appetite

Use up odd scraps of cheese to produce a most inexpensive meal or luxury starter. Soufflés have a reputation for being terribly difficult to cook and serve, but they're not as daunting as they may appear. Soufflés are best eaten immediately from the oven, which can be a bit of a problem with timing, but the main part of the preparation can be done in advance, just leaving the final mixing and baking to do at the last minute. I prefer to make a soufflé in individual ramekin dishes — that way everyone gets a lovely little golden dishful; I feel that with a large dish once the first helping is served, the soufflé collapses and it's a bit of an anti-climax for the rest of the diners!

Preparation and cooking time: 45-50 mins., small dishes
60-65 mins., large dishes

Choose a nice mixture of cheese flavours, according to taste and what is in the fridge, amounting to 3oz/75g cheese altogether. Some suggestions:

2 oz/50g Cheddar with 1 oz/25g Parmesan
2 oz/50g Lancashire with 1 oz/25g Red Leicester
2 oz/50g Stilton with 1 oz/25g Parmesan
2 oz/50g Double Gloucester with 1 oz/25g Stilton

Handful of parsley or watercress or 2 sticks celery (optional)
1 oz/25g butter
1 oz/25g plain flour
¼ pt/150ml milk
Salt, pepper, pinch mustard
3 eggs

Heat oven to 190°C/375°F/gas 5-6, and boil a kettle of water. Grease a 1¾ pt/1 litre soufflé dish or 4 large ramekin dishes.

Finely grate and mix cheeses. Wash and finely snip parsley or watercress or wash, trim and finely chop celery.

Melt butter in a pan over a moderate heat, leave on the heat and add flour, stirring with a wooden spoon, gradually beating in milk to form a smoth paste. Continue to cook for 2-3 mins., stirring all the time, until mixture thickens. Stir in cheese, parsley, watercress or celery if used, and season well. Remove from heat. Separate eggs, beat egg yolks and beat gradually into the flour mixture. The mixture can be set aside at this point until you are ready to complete the dish.

Beat egg whites until stiff and fold them into the cheese mixture using a metal spoon, taking great care not to burst the air bubbles in the egg white. Pour gently into the large soufflé dish or spoon carefully between the small dishes. Pour 1"/2½cm hot water into a large baking tin, carefully stand the soufflé dishes in it, and place in the pre-heated oven. Bake for 20-25 mins., small dishes; 40-45 mins., large dish or until well risen and golden brown. Serve at once, garnished with parsley or watercress.

For a real touch of luxury, dribble double cream over the soufflé just before putting it on the table.

Leftover lightly cooked veg. can be hidden in the soufflé dish before cooking to give a surprise filling. Allow approx. 1 dsp veg. per person — cauliflower or broccoli sprigs, courgette rings, carrot sticks, or tiny raw mushrooms or finely sliced large ones with a dab of butter will cook with the soufflé. Put veg. into the greased dish and cover with the soufflé mixture, then cook as above.

Suzie, my 'daughter-in-law' makes huge individual cheese soufflés, using 2 to 3 eggs each, for a quick luxury supper.

BLUE CHEESE PÂTÉ   *Serves 2*

Use up the remnants of the Christmas Stilton or any bits of blue cheese left in the fridge, mixed with either low calorie curd cheese or cream cheese. The pâté will keep overnight in the fridge, or can be frozen and defrosted before use. Serve as a starter or light snack with hot toast or fresh bread, and garnish with lemon wedges accompanied by fresh fruit — apples, pears, nectarines, peaches, grapes, walnuts, celery or watercress.

Preparation time: 5 mins., plus at least 30 mins. chilling time

3 oz/75g blue cheese — Stilton, Danish Blue, as available
4 oz/100g curd cheese or cream cheese
1 tblsp milk
1 tblsp dry white wine or cider
Salt, pepper

Crumble the blue cheese. Put curd or cream cheese into a bowl and beat to a soft cream with milk and wine. Beat in blue cheese and season with salt and pepper. Roll stiff mixture into a sausage shape — use your fingertips, like playing with plasticine. Wrap in plastic film and chill in fridge for at least half an hour.

To serve: cut pâté into slices or wedges, garnish with fruit and serve with thin toast or bread rolls and butter.

ANNABEL'S CHEESE FONDUE   *Serves 2*

You don't need a special occasion to enjoy a fondue. This is one of my daughter's favourite recipes. It makes a nice cosy supper for two in the winter, or is equally good for a leisurely light lunch in the summer — you can even eat it outside on a hot, still day. It's a good way of using up odds and ends of cheese to make a cheap meal. Fondue is easiest to make in a proper fondue pot with a burner underneath to keep it warm, but cheese fondue will work very well made in a small, thick saucepan without a burner, as it does not need to be kept boiling like an oil fondue; put it on a hotplate if you have one. The fondue will reheat over a very, very low heat if necessary, and you can use forks instead of fondue sticks.

Preparation and cooking time: 20 mins.

1 French stick or 4-5 fresh bread rolls
1 clove fresh garlic
8 oz/225g cheese — a mixture of Gruyère and Emmental is

traditional, but you can substitute the much cheaper
Cheddar, Edam or whatever cheese you have left over
2 tsp cornflour or flour
¼ pt/150ml/1 cup dry white wine or cider (or use
non-alcoholic wine or apple juice if you prefer)
1 tsp lemon juice
1 tsp herb or whole grain mustard
Plenty of black pepper

Cut bread into large bite-sized chunks and put in a serving dish.

Peel garlic, cut it in half and crush or rub it well around base
and sides of fondue pot, to leave a good garlicky flavour. Discard
garlic pieces.

Grate cheeses. Put cornflour or flour into a cup and mix to
a smooth paste with 2-3 tblsp of chosen wine, cider or apple juice.
Put remaining liquid into fondue pot, add lemon juice and heat
gently over a low heat, gradually stirring in the grated cheese
and mustard with a wooden spoon, stirring until all the cheese
has melted. Remove from heat, stir cornflour mixture again, then
mix it into the fondue. Return pot to the heat and cook fondue,
stirring all the time until it is thick, smooth and just bubbling
— the heat must remain turned down low all the time.

Season well with black pepper and carefully carry fondue pot
to the serving table and place over burner if you have one, or
on a hotplate or thick table mat. Always use the correct fuel
recommended for your burner (generally methylated spirit) and
put burner in place before lighting. Never carry a lighted
burner from kitchen to table.

Eat fondue at once, spearing the bread cubes and dipping them
into the hot cheese — it's a more filling meal than you might
expect. My family like fondue served with a few crudités (sticks
of cucumber, carrot, celery, pepper strips, cauliflower florets,
radishes, sliced mushrooms, etc.) or a crunchy salad, to off-set

the richness of the cheese.

P.S. A bottle of dry white wine makes a good accompaniment too!

CHEESE PASTRY   *8 oz/225g pastry*

A very good way of using up bits of cheese, as the pastry is best made with rather dry cheese or it can become too sticky. A strong cheese gives a better flavour (the mild cheese flavour seems to disappear when cooked), or you can add a tblsp grated Parmesan cheese for extra 'bite'.

Preparation time: 10 mins.

8 oz/225g flour
Pinch salt, shake black pepper, shake cayenne pepper
4 oz/100g butter or margarine (block type is best)
3-4 oz/75-100g finely grated hard type cheese — Cheddar, etc.
1 tblsp grated Parmesan cheese (optional)
1-2 egg yolks
Pinch dry mustard or ½ tsp made mustard
Water to mix

Sieve flour, salt, black and cayenne pepper into a mixing bowl or put into a mixer or processor. Cut butter or margarine into small pieces and rub in to flour mixture with fingertips or process until mixture looks like breadcrumbs. Stir in grated cheeses. Beat egg yolks with mustard and stir into mixture, adding enough cold water to make a stiff pastry dough, being careful not to get mixture too wet.

Roll out dough on a lightly floured surface and use as required. If pastry is difficult to roll (being rich, it may be a bit crumbly), make it into a ball, wrap in plastic film or foil and chill in fridge for 30 mins. before rolling out.

Use cheese pastry for savoury pies, meat or vegetable pasties, flans, sausage rolls, cheese straws, cheese biscuits, etc.

CHEESE PASTRY SAUSAGE ROLLS

Makes 6 large
12-18 small

Make tiny sausage rolls to hand round with drinks as a party savoury, or larger ones for a packed lunch or to serve with baked beans or salad for tea or supper.

Preparation and cooking time: 1 hour tiny rolls
1¼ hours large rolls

8 oz/225g cheese pastry − see opposite
8 oz/225g sausage meat or de-skinned sausages
1 tsp mixed dried herbs
Handful fresh snipped parsley
½ small onion, finely chopped
Extra flour for rolling
Milk for brushing

Heat oven to 200°C/400°F/gas 6-7.
 Make pastry, and roll out into an oblong approx. 12"/30cm × 8"/20cm. Cut in half longways.
 Put sausage meat into a basin, mash in herbs, parsley and onion. Divide in half, and using a little flour on your hands, roll into two long sausages, to fit length of pastry. Place sausage on one side of pastry, brush edge with milk and roll pastry over to enclose sausage, ending up with the 'seam' underneath. Press firmly to close and cut each sausage into required lengths (cut into 3 or 4 for large rolls, 6-9 for party nibbles). Put onto a baking tray, seams underneath, and shape neatly. Brush tops with milk, make 2 or 3 slits on top of each roll and bake in the hot oven

for 10-15 mins., until pastry starts to colour. Reduce heat to 180°C/350°F/gas 4-5 and cook for a further 10-15 mins. (small rolls) or 15-20 mins. (large rolls) until pastry is crisp and golden and sausage meat is cooked.

Serve hot from the oven, or cool on a wire tray and store in the fridge, reheating for 5-10 mins. in a hot oven before serving. Sausage rolls freeze well and can be defrosted when needed and served hot as above.

7 MILK

Sometimes you seem to accumulate pints of milk in the fridge — easily done if you've had a houseful of people and extra milk at the weekend, then forgot to change the order for Monday morning when they've all gone back to work or school!

Milk freezes well, provided of course that it is fresh when put into the freezer; don't freeze milk that's been lurking at the back of the fridge for a week — use that up in a big batch of scones and freeze them for later. Pour fresh milk from glass bottles into plastic containers or plastic bottles (the kind fizzy drinks are sold in work well, but empty squash bottles usually carry the smell of orange or lemon so don't use those), and put into the freezer, taking care that bottles are upright until the milk is frozen. Leave space in plastic bottles for expansion of the milk when frozen, and *do not freeze milk in glass bottles* as they may crack as the milk expands at low temperatures. Defrost at room temperature, in the fridge or in the microwave (remember to remove any metal tops), stir well and use as fresh milk.

During my wartime childhood (no fridges then in many households), on cold winter days my mother would leave the bottles of milk outside to freeze, then carefully spoon off the frozen milk into little bowls and top it with a large spoonful of condensed milk! My brother and I thought it was the height of luxury and it tasted particularly good if we were lucky enough to be given the full cream milk! Today's children, used to the ice-cream van, are perhaps too sophisticated for this, but it may still have novelty value.

There are lots of savoury meats, fish and vegetable dishes that involve using a white or cheese sauce, and lots and lots of puds that will soon use up that spare milk. Or why not spoil yourself on a cold evening with a rich, boozy egg nog or a super summer milk shake on a hot summer day?

Recipes using ¼ pt/150ml milk

Beefy Bullets (p. 25)
Coffee, Iced (p. 117)
  — per person
Mixed Cheese Soufflé
  (p. 105)
Poor Knights' Pudding
  (p. 134)

Chocolate, Luxury Hot
  (p. 118) — per person
Milk Shakes, Summer
  (p. 116)
  — ⅓ pt/200ml per person
Potato Supper
  (p. 77)

Recipes using ½ pt/300ml milk

Bread "Pudden" (p. 129)
Chicken & Ham Gougère
  (p. 50)
Drinking Egg or Boozy Egg
  Nog (p. 115)
Quick Savoury Pancakes
  (p. 30)
Vegetable Gougère (p. 75)

Cauliflower Savoury (p. 74)
Creamed Chicken Mornay
  (p. 52)
Monday Moussaka (p. 34)
Quiche Lorraine (p. 91)
Savoury Flan (p. 79)
Toad In The Hole (p. 31)
Vol-au-Vents (p. 51)

Recipes using 1 pint/600ml milk

Bread & Butter Pudding (p. 129)

Real Rice Pudding (p. 133)

Magic Islands (p. 135)

Queen's Pudding (p. 132)

Tidy Up Trifle (p. 138)

Recipe using yoghurt

Nutty Mushroom Pasta (p. 85)

DRINKING EGG OR BOOZY EGG NOG

1 large glassful

A quick, nourishing 'meal' for those in a hurry. My children used to love a frothy, sweet drinking egg served in a posh glass with a straw when they weren't feeling too well, but nowadays you should check with your doctor before serving raw eggs to children or invalids.

Preparation time: 5 mins.

1 egg
1-3 tsp sugar
½ pt/300ml milk (cold or warm)
1 tblsp sherry)
Good "slurp" brandy, rum or whisky) **optional**
Pinch of nutmeg or cinnamon
** or a sprinkle of drinking chocolate**

Break egg into a basin, beat it lightly with a mixer, whisk or fork, adding the sugar and gradually beating in the milk to produce a good froth! Add sherry and spirits if used. Pour into a tall glass, sprinkle with spice or drinking chocolate, and serve at once.

SUMMER MILK SHAKES

Absolutely gorgeous to enjoy in the garden on a hot summer day. Serve in big glasses with bright bendy straws. You need a liquidiser or processor to make really frothy milk shakes.

Preparation time: 5 mins.

For each milk shake allow:
⅓ pt/200ml cold milk
1-2 large scoops ice-cream — vanilla, chocolate, coffee, strawberry, etc. to complement the chosen flavouring

Suggested flavourings:
½ tsp vanilla essence
1 heaped tsp instant coffee powder or 1 tsp 'Camp' coffee liquid
3-4 tsp drinking chocolate
1 tblsp milk shake cordial in various fruit flavours
1 ripe banana, cut into pieces
Few fresh strawberries, sliced

Boozy flavours — adults only:
1-2 tblsp crème de cacao
1-2 tblsp rum
1-2 tblsp amaretto

Toppings:
Small scoop ice-cream
Dribble of pouring cream, spoonful of whipped cream or gorgeous big swirl of aerosol cream
Dusting of drinking chocolate or grated chocolate for chocolate, coffee or vanilla flavours
Fresh fruit — strawberry, raspberries, sliced peaches, etc. for fruit flavours
Chocolate flake bar — banana, chocolate or vanilla flavour

To serve: **ice cubes (optional)**

Put milk in liquidiser or processor (it should be chilled from
the fridge). Add large scoop ice-cream and chosen flavouring
and whizz for a few moments — it shouldn't be completely
smooth; a few lumps of ice-cream look nice. Pour into a large
glass (chill glass in fridge if liked, or pour milk over small
ice cubes), top with a little more ice-cream and cream if
liked. Decorate with fresh fruit or chocolate flake, dust with
chocolate if used and serve at once with a bendy straw and a
cocktail umbrella if liked!

ICED COFFEE

I sometimes serve iced coffee with lots of chocolate mints
instead of a dessert after an informal lunch on a hot, sunny day,
but it's delicious any time.

For each person allow:
**1 small coffee cup (posh after-dinner size) strong black coffee
 — strong ground coffee or double strength instant — chilled
 in the fridge**
¼ pt/150ml cold milk
1 large scoop coffee ice-cream
1-2 tblsp rum (optional)

Toppings:
Small scoop coffee ice-cream
Dribble of pouring cream, whipped cream or aerosol cream
Chocolate flake, grated chocolate or drinking chocolate
1 tblsp chopped mixed nuts or a few flaked almonds

To serve: **ice cubes (optional)**

Make double strength black coffee and chill in fridge. When
cold, put coffee, cold milk, ice-cream and rum, if used, into

liquidiser or processor, and whizz for a few moments. Pour ice cubes into cold glasses and pour frothy coffee mixture over. Top with small scoops ice-cream, decorate with cream, chocolate and/or nuts and serve at once.

LUXURY HOT CHOCOLATE

Lovely and comforting on a nasty cold evening or after a long country walk in the winter.

Preparation and cooking time: 5 mins.

2-3 squares chocolate (optional)
½ pt/300ml milk
1 tblsp drinking chocolate
3 or 4 marshmallows (optional)

Toppings:
1 tblsp pouring cream, whipped cream or aerosol cream
Shake of drinking chocolate or grated chocolate (or
    both!)
Chocolate flake (optional)
1 or 2 marshmallows (optional)

Break chocolate squares, if used, into a mug. Heat milk to almost boiling point and pour into mug, add drinking chocolate and marshmallows, if used, and stir until dissolved. Top with cream and decorate with drinking or grated chocolate, chocolate flake and halved marshmallows, if liked. Serve at once, while lovely and hot.

8 MAINLY FRUIT

While perhaps not strictly leftovers (apart from the odd spoonful of apple sauce or the bits of fruit salad that nobody ate) fruit can easily be a surplus. The fruit which ripens in everyone's gardens all at the same time, the bananas quietly going brown in the fruit bowl and the half melon in the fridge all need using up and dealing with immediately if they are not to go to waste.

If you're lucky enough to have a regular glut of fresh fruit each year, the easiest solution is freezing — most fruits will freeze either fresh or cooked, and can be stashed away for use later when they are more expensive or unobtainable. I'm not a very happy jam or marmalade maker — the memory of burning a huge pan of oranges when at college and having to scour the preserving pan back to pristine condition good enough to satisfy the cookery tutor is still painful thirty years on — but freezer raspberry jam (p. 124) is so simple to make (takes no cooking), that even I can enjoy making it, and it tastes absolutely marvellous.

Apples

Peel, slice, cook and purée. Freeze in plastic containers (margarine tubs of various sizes) in suitable amounts for your family, ready to sweeten and use in pies, crumble, sauce, apple snow, etc. If you can't be bothered with all that cooking, peel and slice apples, open freeze on trays, then store in a large plastic container (ice-cream tub). The slices may brown slightly, but it won't show when they are cooked later, especially if you use brown sugar to sweeten. Do not add sugar before freezing, as different dishes require differing amounts of sweetening.

Recipes using apples

Chinese Chicken (p. 45)   Christmas Pie (p. 37)
Coleslaw (p. 95)   Ki's Apple Snow (p. 147)
Norwegian Apple Crisp (p. 137) — 1½ lb-2 lb/750-100g
Nutty Apple & Blackberry Charlotte (p. 131)
Salad, Boxing Day (p. 48)
Tomato Chutney, Mahshar (p. 125) — 1 lb/450g

Bananas

Make banana sandwiches with fresh brown bread and butter, spread with mashed banana and honey or brown sugar. Serve bananas for a quick dessert with ice-cream, cream, chocolate sauce and a sprinkle of nuts or grated chocolate.

Recipes using bananas

Summer Milk Shakes (p. 116) Yummy Banana Bread (p. 151)

Blackberries

Spread out on a tray and open freeze, then pack into plastic tubs or polythene bags. If you are picking just a few from the garden each day, they will freeze satisfactorily if just dropped into a plastic tub in the freezer until you eventually have a tubful.

To make blackberry purée — simmer for a few minutes in a little water until soft, then liquidise or process, sieve to get rid

of the pips and freeze in suitable-sized containers for use in fruit
fool (see p. 145), or as a sauce poured over ice-cream and fresh
or canned fruit. Sweeten to taste after defrosting.

Recipes using blackberries

Fruit Fool (p. 145)   Norwegian Apple Crisp
Nutty Apple & Blackberry   (p. 137)
  Charlotte (p. 137)   Super Summer Pudding (p. 144)

Red- and blackcurrants

Top, tail, wash, drain well and open freeze. Pour into a large
plastic tub ready to use in pies or crumble, or to add colour to
fruit salad, pavlova or fruit cheesecake, etc.

Recipes using red/blackcurrants

Norwegian Apple Crisp   Super Summer Pudding
  (p. 137)   (p. 144)

Gooseberries

Wash, cook in a very little water, purée in a liquidiser or
processor, and sieve; no need to top and tail as the bits will be
removed in the sieving. If you want whole fruit for pies: top and
tail fruit, wash, drain and open freeze, then pour into a large
polythene tub or double polythene bag and store until needed.
They can be defrosted or cooked from frozen.

Recipe using gooseberries

Fruit Fool (p. 145)

Recipe using peaches

Summer Milk Shakes (p. 116)

Plums

I'm lucky enough to have a generous neighbour with a fantastic plum tree, so when we've eaten all we can face, I wash and open freeze the plums on a tray, then pour them into a plastic tub or double polythene bag. They freeze as hard as bullets, but will defrost or cook from frozen, and are excellent in pies and crumbles or topped with the crispy, sweet breadcrumb topping (p. 99).

Raspberries

Wash if you like, but be careful not to break the berries, open freeze on trays and then store carefully in a large plastic tub.

Purée fresh raspberries by mashing slightly with a fork or potato masher, and freeze in small plastic tubs ready to mix with whipped cream for instant dessert.

Recipes using raspberries

Fruit Fool (p. 145)

Sarah's Mum's Freezer
  Raspberry Jam (p. 124)

Tidy Up Trifle (p. 138)

Norwegian Apple Crisp (p. 137)

Summer Milk Shakes (p. 116)

Super Summer Pudding
  (p. 144)

Rhubarb

Peel if necessary, cut into 1-2″/2½-5cm lengths and open freeze. Store in plastic tubs and use for pies, crumbles, or purée and make into fruit fool mixed with whipped cream.

Strawberries

These do not freeze whole very successfully (they go soggy when defrosted), so I wash, hull and mush them about a bit or purée not too finely, and freeze in small plastic tubs to use in mousse or as strawberry sauce for pud and ice-cream. Fresh or frozen strawberry purée makes lovely strawberry milk shakes, with cold milk and ice-cream, whizzed in the liquidiser for a few moments.

Recipes using strawberriesa

Fruit Fool (p. 145)   Sarah's Mum's Freezer
Summer Milk Shakes   Raspberry Jam (p. 124)
  (p. 116)   Super Summer Pudding
Tidy Up Trifle (p. 138)   (p. 144)

Odds and Ends

Small amounts of cooked fruit can be used in pie or pasty fillings, or mixed with other complementary fruit in larger pies, crumbles, etc., or can be frozen for later use. Small amounts of tinned fruit or fruit salad can be used in trifle (see p. 138) or added to an exotic fruit cocktail or Pimms — you deserve one after all that cooking!

And extra vegetables

Mushrooms

Wipe or wash and drain well, and open freeze on flat trays. Pack carefully (they're a bit brittle) into a plastic box or plastic bags. I think they're a bit soft if defrosted and grilled, but they're fine for use in meat or vegetable casseroles, vegetarian dishes, sauces, soups, or fried gently from frozen (delicious fried in butter and garlic and served on toast for a lunchtime snack).

Tomatoes

Best made into Italian Tomato Sauce (see p. 126) and frozen in suitable-sized containers, or used to make Mahshar Tomato Chutney which uses red or green tomatoes (see p. 125).

In an emergency, quarter washed tomatoes and open freeze on trays, then pack into a plastic tub to use later from frozen for sauces or in casseroles or in vegetarian dishes (no need to defrost before cooking). Tomatoes can even be frozen whole if you're really short of time; they will resemble golf balls, but can be used in cooking as needed.

SARAH'S MUM'S FREEZER RASPBERRY JAM
Six-seven 1 lb/500g jars

My daughter Annabel first tasted this jam at her school friend Sarah's house and begged the recipe from Sarah's mum. It's the most gorgeous jam I've ever made. As it doesn't need cooking, the full flavour of the fruit is left in the jar — and it's so easy to make, no bubbling and burning preserving pans, just a big mixing bowl of fruit and sugar. The jam must be stored in the freezer, then kept in the fridge once opened.

Preparation time: 10 mins. Standing time: 1 hour

2½ lb/1100g raspberries
4 lb/1800g sugar
8 oz/225g jar liquid pectin (Certo, available at supermarkets and chemists)
4 tblsp lemon juice
6-7 clean, dry jam jars with lids and/or jam papers

Wash and drain fruit, tip into a large mixing bowl and mash gently with a wooden spoon, potato masher or fork. Stir in sugar, mix well and leave for about 1 hour at room temperature, until the sugar has completely dissolved, stirring once or twice. Add pectin and lemon juice and stir continuously for about 2 mins. to mix really well.

Pour or ladle into clean, dry jam jars, leaving ½"/1cm headroom. Cover with jam papers and/or lids. Leave for 48 hours at room temperature, then keep at least one jar in the fridge for immediate use and store the rest in the freezer. Defrost for about 2 hours at room temperature before use.

I've tried this recipe using strawberries, and although the jam has a lovely flavour it remains very runny and will not set. However, it makes a delicious sauce for ice-cream, iced desserts or sponge puds, or as a base for mousse or homemade ice-cream, mixed with whipped cream.

MAHSHAR TOMATO CHUTNEY

Approx. six 1 lb/500g jars

I first made this chutney when we lived in a rather primitive area of Iran, where the tomatoes came in all manner of colours, shapes and sizes, the onions varied from white to deep mauve and the dates were fresh off the trees — even there it tasted good!

Preparation and cooking time: 1-1¼ hours, best kept at least 2-3 months before use.

1 lb/500g tomatoes — red or green
1 lb/500g eating and/or cooking apples
1 lb/500g onions
½ lb/250g dates (use seedless raisins or sultanas if preferred)
1 lb/500g brown sugar
1 level tblsp salt
½ tsp cayenne pepper
1-2 tsp pickling spices (tie these in a muslin bag if you prefer not to have them in the finished chutney)
½ pt/300ml malt vinegar

Wash and chop tomatoes, peel, core and chop apples, peel and chop onions, stone and slice dates or wash raisins or sultanas if used. Put everything into a large enamel or suitably coated saucepan (not aluminium or metal as that would react badly with the vinegar), add sugar, salt, cayenne pepper, pickling spices and vinegar, and bring slowly to the boil, stirring gently. Reduce heat and simmer for approx. 30 mins., stirring occasionally until veg. are soft and chutney has formed a nice, soft, saucy consistency.

Cool slightly, remove muslin bag of spices, then pour or ladle carefully into clean jam or preserving jars, leaving a tiny space between chutney and lid (do not use metal lids as the vinegar could corrode the metal). Allow to cool, then cover with suitable lids or jam papers, label and date jars and store in a cool place for 2-3 months to allow the delicious flavour to develop fully as the chutney matures.

This chutney is nice after Christmas with cold turkey, ham or other cold meats.

ITALIAN TOMATO SAUCE

Makes a generous pint/600ml

If you (or your neighbours) grow tomatoes, you'll be well aware that for ages you're waiting for the fruit to ripen, then suddenly it's all ready at once, and everyone is offering their friends "a bag of lovely fresh toms". I make double or treble quantity of this sauce (sometimes mixing fresh and canned tomatoes if I haven't quite enough) and freeze it in single portions (about ¼ pt/150ml/1 cup), to defrost as required. It's useful as a base for Bolognese sauce, good with spaghetti or other pasta, lasagne, moussaka, meat, fish or vegetable dishes, or as a gravy for the vegetarian when the rest of the family is eating a meat meal.

Preparation and cooking time: 30-40 mins.

2 large onions
2 cloves garlic or ½ tsp garlic granules or paste
2 tblsp oil (olive or walnut oil give the best flavour)
1 lb/500g fresh, ripe tomatoes — or mix with canned tomatoes
2 tblsp tomato purée or ketchup
1-2 dried Italian tomatoes in oil (optional)
1 tsp sugar

1 tsp mixed herbs
Salt, black pepper
Dash of soy, tabasco or Worcester sauce (omit for vegetarians)

Peel and finely chop onions and fresh garlic. Heat oil in a saucepan over a moderate heat and fry onion and garlic gently for 4-5 mins. until soft but not brown. Wash and chop fresh tomatoes and add to the onion, with canned tomatoes and juice if used. Stir in tomato purée or ketchup, chopped sun-dried tomatoes, sugar and herbs, and season to taste with salt, pepper and chosen sauces. Bring to the boil over a moderate heat, stirring well, and add half a cup of water if the sauce seems too thick. Reduce heat and simmer for 10-15 mins., (20-25 mins. if making double quantity), stirring occasionally, until thick and soft.

Cool slightly, then liquidise or process to make a smooth sauce, or leave if you prefer a rougher texture. Adjust seasoning and use as required, or pour into suitable containers and freeze. This sauce cooks, defrosts and reheats very well in the microwave oven.

9 PUDDINGS, DESSERTS & CAKES

I'm putting puds, desserts and cakes all together for easy reference, but they are also listed in the appropriate chapters according to the main ingredient.

Most of the puds and cakes are extraordinarily cheap and easy to make — adapt the basic recipe to use up whatever oddments you have in the fridge or larder — they'll be different, taste delicious and be even better if there's a little leftover cream to accompany them!

The hot puds can be quickly assembled and popped in the oven to give a 'comfort eating' treat on a cold day, or to pad out a light main course, while the cold desserts and cakes are a treat at any time.

BREAD "PUDDEN" *Serves 4-6*

A good way of using up stale bread, very quick to prepare but allow time for bread to soak.

Preparation and cooking time: 1¼ hours, plus 30 mins. soaking

8 oz/225g stale bread — brown, white or a mixture
½ pt/300ml milk
4-6 oz/100-150g mixed dried fruit
4 oz/100g sugar
2 oz/50g butter (nicer than marg.)
1 egg
1-2 tsp mixed spice
Pinch grated nutmeg

Break bread into small pieces, put into a mixing bowl and cover with the milk. Stir well and leave to soak for about 30 mins., until bread has soaked up milk.

Heat oven to 180°C/350°F/gas 4-5, well grease a 2½ pt/1½ litre oven-proof pie dish.

Wash and drain dried fruit and stir into soaked bread and milk, with the sugar and butter chopped into little pieces. Beat egg in a small basin with the spice and stir into the pudding, mixing well. Pour mixture into the greased dish, sprinkle with a little more grated nutmeg. Bake in the moderate oven for 50-60 mins. until set.

Serve hot or cold, on its own or with cream or custard.

BREAD AND BUTTER PUDDING *Serves 4*

This is *the* leftovers pud that everyone either loves or loathes. This recipe gives a delicious tasty pud with a nice crispy top

(I leave the crusts on for extra crunch). With all the eggs and milk in the recipe it makes a good dish to serve after a lighter or vegetarian first course. It can also make a good supper dish — much more interesting than poached egg on toast with a glass of milk!

Preparation and cooking time: 1 hour plus 30 mins. soaking

6 slices bread (large loaf)
3 oz/75g butter (nicer than margarine), softened
3-4 oz/75-100g currants or sultanas
2 oz/50g sugar
2 eggs
1 pt/½ litre milk
½ tsp vanilla essence

Well grease a 2½ pt/1½ litre deep pie or oven-proof dish. Remove crusts from bread if you wish, and butter bread. Cut slices into triangles and arrange a layer of bread on the base of the dish, butter side down, sprinkle with half of the washed drained currants or sultanas and sprinkle with a tblsp sugar. Cover with another layer of bread, sprinkle with the rest of the fruit and another tblsp sugar. Top with rest of the bread, butter side up and sprinkle with remaining sugar. Beat eggs, mix in milk and essence and pour over pud. Leave to soak for about 30 mins. or longer, until the bread has nearly soaked up all the milk.

Heat the oven to 170°C/325°F/gas 3-4. Bake pud in the moderate oven for 40-45 mins. until set with a lovely golden crispy top.

Serve hot, on its own or with thick cream.

NUTTY APPLE & BLACKBERRY CHARLOTTE

Serves 4-6

A good quick pud to make when there are windfall apples about and the blackberries are plentiful. Even quicker to make if you have breadcrumbs ready made in the freezer.

Preparation and cooking time: 1 hour approx.

Topping:
6 oz/150g fresh breadcrumbs, white or brown
4 oz/100g shredded suet
4 oz/100g demerara or granulated sugar
3 oz/75g mixed chopped nuts

1½ lb-2 lb/700-1000g cooking apples and blackberries, mixed as available
3-4 oz/75-100g sugar, or to taste

Heat oven to 190°C/375°F/gas 5-6.

Mix breadcrumbs, suet, sugar and nuts for topping. Peel, core and thinly slice apples, wash and drain blackberries. Well grease a 2½ pt/1½ litre deep ovenproof dish and put in half the apples, cover with half the blackberries and sprinkle on half the sugar. Cover with half the topping. Repeat layers, using up all the ingredients and fork the top neatly. Bake in the hot oven for 40-45 mins., until fruit is cooked and top is crisp and golden.

Serve hot or cold, with cream, ice-cream or custard.

This pud can be made using any cooking fruit — plums, rhubarb, apricots, raspberries, etc. — any mixture you have available.

QUEEN'S PUDDING
Serves 4-6

Use up the heel of the loaf or the last few slices in the packet, and make an old fashioned 'Sunday Dinner' treat. Don't be put off by all the timings below, it's very easy to prepare.

Base — Preparation and soaking time: 35 mins.
        Cooking time: 25-30 mins.
Meringue — Preparation and cooking time: 25-35 mins.

Base: **4 oz/100g/4 thick slices bread**
             1 pt/600ml milk
             1 oz/25g butter or margarine
             Grated rind 1 lemon or 1 tsp vanilla essence
             2 oz/50g sugar
             3 eggs yolks
             **3-4 tblsp jam — raspberry or strawberry is
               traditional but apricot is delicious**
Meringue: **3 egg whites***
             6 heaped tblsp sugar
             3-4 glacé cherries and angelica to decorate

Make breadcrumbs (use a blender or grater), put them into a bowl. Heat milk, butter or marg., lemon rind or vanilla essence and sugar over a gentle heat, stirring until sugar is dissolved. Pour warm mixture over breadcrumbs, stir and leave to soak for 20-25 mins. to allow crumbs to absorb milk.

Heat the oven to 170°C/325°F/gas 3-4.

Beat egg yolks and beat into bread mixture. Pour into a well greased 2½ pt/1½ litre deep pie or oven-proof dish, and bake in the moderate oven for 25-30 mins. until set. Remove from heat and spread top with jam — warm jar of jam by standing it in a little hot water if jam is too stiff to spread easily.

Lower oven heat to 150°C/300°F/gas 2-3. Make meringues — beat egg whites until stiff using a mixer or processor. Beat in sugar 2 tsp at a time until meringue is thick and all the sugar is beaten in (mixture will hold stiff peaks when heaped up). Pile meringue on top of pud, covering base completely. Decorate with pieces of glacé cherries and angelica if liked.

Bake in the low oven for 20-30 mins., until meringue is firm and lightly coloured on top. It's nicest served warm, on its own or with cream.

If time is short the meringue may be flashed into a hot oven, 200°C/400°F/gas 6-7 for 3-5 mins., until meringue is firm and just coloured, but the pudding must be served while still hot, as the soft meringue won't keep crisp for long.

Do not store any leftover pud in the fridge, as the meringue will 'weep', and do not freeze as the custard will separate (in fact, it's the sort of pud which really does need to be finished up at one meal!).

*Spare egg whites can be whisked up with the rest of the whites adding 2 tblsp sugar for each extra white, to give a really snowy (and showy!) pud.

REAL RICE PUDDING   *Serves 3-4*

A proper rice pudding with skin on! The preparation time only takes a few moments, then you can put the pud in the oven and leave it.

Preparation and cooking time: 1¾-2 hours

3 oz/75g pudding (round Carolina) rice
2 oz/50g sugar
1 pt/600ml milk*
1 oz/25g butter

(continued overleaf)

(Real Rice Pudding continued)

Pinch grated nutmeg or mixed spice
*For a really rich pudding use ¾pt/450ml milk mixed with
¼pt/150ml cream or evaporated milk

Heat oven to 160°C/325°F/gas 3-4.

Well grease a 2 pt/1¼ litre deep oven-proof or pie dish. Put
rice, sugar and milk (and cream if used) into the dish and stir
well. Dot with butter, sprinkle with grated nutmeg or mixed
spice and bake for 1¾-2 hours — the pud will cook quite
happily left to its own devices in the low oven. Serve the
pudding warm from the oven, with pouring cream if you feel
really self-indulgent, or a large dollop of soft vanilla ice-cream.

Children (and some adults) often appreciate a spoonful of red
jam in the middle (to stir the pudding into the most disgusting
shade of pink), and my father likes rice pud cooked with a
handful of washed currants or sultanas stirred into the pud with
the sugar, before cooking.

If you make a larger pudding you must allow a longer cooking
time — up to 4 hours for a big pudding.

The Scandinavians make a huge 'rice porridge' to be eaten as
part of their traditional Christmas Eve meal. An almond is
hidden in the pud, and whoever finds it is King or Queen of the
feast, and is assured of good luck, health and happiness in the
coming year.

POOR KNIGHTS' PUDDING   *Serves 2*

Those knights knew a thing or two — maybe they made this at
the end of the week when the king was a bit late with the wage
cheques! It may be cheap but it's delicious and filling, a
sophisticated version of the boarding school favourite, eggy
bread. Use up any kind of bread — brown, white or leftover jam
or honey sandwiches, or make the French 'Pain Perdu', using
rounds of French bread. The knights undoubtedly used dripping

or lard for frying, but a mixture of oil and butter will please the health-conscious modern taste.

Preparation and cooking time: 20 mins.

**2-6 thick slices of bread (brown, white or French), according
  to size, or 4-8 jam or honey sandwiches**
1 egg plus an extra yolk if it's spare
¼ pt/150ml milk
½ glass sherry or brandy (optional)
2-3 tsp sugar to taste
3-4 tblsp oil with 1 oz/25g butter for frying

Topping: **1-2 tblsp sugar, left plain or mixed with 1 tsp
           cinnamon, nutmeg or mixed spice as preferred.**

Cut crusts off bread and cut into dainty sandwich-sized triangles or squares, or make small jam or honey sandwiches and put into a shallow dish.

Put egg, and extra yolk if used, into a basin and beat well, beating in milk, sherry or brandy, and sugar to taste. Pour egg mixture over bread and leave for a few minutes to soak. Turn bread over carefully and leave for a few more minutes until all the egg is soaked into the bread. Heat oil and butter in large frying pan over a moderate heat until just hazing, and, using a fish slice, carefully put the soaked bread slices into the hot fat. Cook for a few moments until golden, then turn and cook the other side. Drain on kitchen paper and serve on a warm plate, dredged with the prepared sugar.

MAGIC ISLANDS   *Serves 4*

An unusual dessert, popular with children and sophisticated enough for grown-ups. Useful for using up the extra milk you forgot to cancel.

Preparation and cooking time: 25 mins. plus cooling time

Islands:	**2 egg whites**
	2 oz/50g sugar
Custard:	**1 pt/600ml milk**
	2 eggs plus 2 egg yolks
	2 oz/50g sugar
	1 tsp cornflour
	½ tsp vanilla essence

Kitchen paper for draining
A plainer custard can be made using just the 2 egg yolks
and 1 tblsp cornflour, instead of the two whole eggs and
1 tsp cornflour

Make meringue islands — whisk egg whites in a large bowl using a whisk, electric mixer or processor, until thick. Then gradually beat in sugar, 1 tsp at a time, to make a stiff meringue mixture.

Pour milk into a really large saucepan or a very clean frying pan and heat milk gently until warm but not boiling. Slide large spoonfuls of meringue onto the milk and poach over a very low heat for 4-5 mins. until set — allow 1 large or 2 small islands each. Carefully lift out cooked islands with a slotted spoon or fish slice and leave to drain on kitchen paper.

Make custard using the warm milk — blend whole eggs, egg yolks, sugar, cornflour and vanilla essence in a basin and beat until smooth with a wooden spoon. Add the warm milk from the pan, stirring hard. Return mixture to the pan, and heat very, very gently, stirring continuously until mixture thickens — *do not let it boil or it will curdle*. If you prefer, cook custard in a double boiler or a basin standing in a saucepan with 2″/5cm hot water over a moderate heat, and stir until mixture thickens.

Pour cooked custard into a wide, heat-proof glass dish and float meringue islands on top. Leave to cool, but this pud is nicest just warm, not chilled in the fridge.

NORWEGIAN APPLE CRISP   *Serves 4-6*

Very economical, and you can use up any spare breadcrumbs in the freezer and apple purée made from windfalls or pre-frozen in the autumn when apples are cheap (or free!). Ring the changes by adding a handful of cooked blackberries, red- or blackcurrants or crushed raspberries to the apple.

Preparation and cooking time: 15-30 mins.
                         plus 30 mins. chilling time

1½ lb-2 lb/700-1000g cooking apples plus a cup of soft fruit
   if liked
1 lemon
1-2 tblsp cold water, white wine or dry cider
3-4 oz/75-100g sugar, or to taste
4 oz/100g butter or margarine
8 oz/225g soft breadcrumbs, white or brown
3 oz/75g demerara sugar
To serve: **4-6 scoops soft vanilla ice-cream**
             A little whipped or aerosol cream
             Handful flaked almonds or chopped mixed nuts

Peel, core and slice apples, wash soft fruit, wash lemon and cut into quarters. Put fruit (except raspberries, see below) into a pan with lemon, water or booze and simmer for 10-15 mins. until soft. Remove lemon, squash juice from lemon quarters into fruit purée, and discard skin. Mash or process fruit to make a smooth purée, stir in crushed raspberries if used (any other soft fruit may be cooked with the apples or added now) and add sugar to taste. Leave to cool.

   Heat butter in a large frying pan over a moderate heat, and fry breadcrumbs, turning frequently until golden and crunchy. Remove from heat, stir in demerara sugar and leave to cool slightly.

Using individual sundae glasses or a large glass dish (the layers look pretty through the glass), put half the fruit purée into the bottom of the dishes and cover with a layer of breadcrumbs using half the topping. Repeat layers, using up all the ingredients. Put in fridge to chill until needed.

To serve: top each sundae with a scoop of ice-cream (or cover top of large dish with a scoop for each person), decorate with a little whipped cream (the aerosol type is handy for this) and sprinkle with flaked almonds or chopped nuts. Serve at once.

TIDY UP TRIFLE   *Serves 6 or more*

The ultimate store-cupboard meal, useful at the end of a bank holiday when you've got a houseful of children and guests and need yet another pudding! Use up any cake left in the tin, with fruit salad left in the fridge or any tinned or suitable fresh fruit, and make a custard with the extra milk that has accumulated in the fridge. Mix and match layers and ingredients to taste, time available and whether the diners will be adults or children, and produce a pud ranging from the easy 'cake and custard' to an alcoholic extravaganza.

Preparation and setting time: most of the morning

Base: enough cake to cover the base of a trifle bowl, preferably sponge cake, or Swiss roll, but you can use fruit cake or bought trifle sponges if you prefer.
2-3 tblsp jam
2-3 macaroons or a few ratafias, if available
Large sherry-glass sherry, wine (use up the end of the bottle), fruit juice or syrup from canned fruit — orange juice is really nice with a chocolate cake base
Fresh or frozen soft fruit (raspberries, strawberries, etc.), any canned fruit or leftover fruit salad, etc. — enough to spoon over the cake

Jelly: optional — I like it as a layer between the cake and the custard as it looks pretty, but the custard can be poured on top of the fruit. Use 1 jelly, made as instructed on the packet — you may prefer to use just enough jelly to cover the cake and put the rest to set in a separate dish to serve with ice-cream for those who 'hate trifle'.

Custard: Quick and Easy — 2 tblsp custard powder
2-3 tblsp sugar
¾ pt/450ml milk

Instant Whip type — make up as instructed on packet

Proper Trifle Custard — 3 egg yolks
1 heaped tblsp sugar
1 tsp cornflour
few drops vanilla essence
½ pt/300ml milk

Topping — ½ pt/300ml double or whipping cream
1-2 egg whites (optional)
or Dream topping made with   ½ pt/300ml milk
2 tblsp flaked almonds
Few glacé cherries and strips angelica
'Hundreds and thousands' — coloured or chocolate

For goodness' sake don't try to use all the ingredients or even all the layers! Choose what you fancy from the suggestions.

Slice cake in half and spread with jam if used, and put a thick layer of cake into the trifle bowl. Roughly crumble macaroons or ratafias over the top, pour over booze or fruit juice, spoon fruit on top and leave it to soak.

Make jelly according to instructions on packet, using up any juice from the fruit with the water, and leave it in the fridge until cold and semi-set, so that it won't disappear when poured onto the cake. When ready, pour or spoon jelly over trifle, and leave it in the fridge to finish setting.

Make chosen custard:

Quick custard — make as directed on the packet, but use ¾ pt/450ml milk to make a thicker, creamy custard.

Instant whip — make as directed on packet.

Proper Trifle custard — blend egg yolks, sugar, cornflour and vanilla essence in a basin. Heat milk until pleasantly warm but not hot, pour it over egg mixture stirring hard with a wooden spoon. Return mixture to pan and heat very gently until mixture thickens, stirring all the time. *Do not let it boil or custard will curdle.* If preferred, cook custard in a double boiler or stand basin in a large pan with 2"/5cm hot water, stirring well until custard thickens. Leave to cool.

When custard is cool but not set, pour over trifle (make sure it's cold or the jelly will melt), and leave to set. Whip cream until thick. If liked, whip egg whites and fold them carefully into the whipped cream to make a lighter topping, or make up Dream Topping as directed on packet. Spread chosen cream over custard, decorate with almonds, glacé cherries and angelica and chill until ready to serve. If decorating with hundreds and thousands, sprinkle these on at the last minute, as the colour runs if left too long.

Some suggested flavours:

Chocolate cake with orange juice — top with chocolate custard or instant whip and grated chocolate.

Fruit cake and macaroons with sherry — omit fruit and jelly layers and top with proper trifle custard, cream and almonds.

Swiss roll with pineapple juice and fresh or canned pineapple.

PAVLOVA CAKE   *Serves 4-6*

Quite different from the 'normal' Pavlova, which is usually a crisp meringue flan. This is a really soft, gooey meringue, and it can be decorated with fresh cream, fresh or canned fruit, chopped nuts etc., whatever is available. Serve as a pudding or a 'fork' cake for tea or supper.

Preparation and cooking time: 1 hour plus cooling time

3 egg whites
Pinch salt
4 oz/100g sugar
1 heaped tsp cornflour
1 tsp vinegar
½ tsp vanilla essence

Topping: ¼ pt/150ml double or Chantilly cream (see page 149)
1-2 cups fresh or canned fruit — fruit salad, mandarin oranges, pineapple pieces, sliced peaches, seedless grapes, raspberries, strawberries
1-2 tblsp chopped nuts or flaked almonds or
1-2 tblsp grated chocolate

Heat oven to 150°C/300°F/gas 2-3. Line base and sides of an 8″/20cm deep cake tin with greased greaseproof paper or silicone paper.

Beat egg whites and salt in a large bowl until stiff, using a whisk, mixer or processor. Gradually beat in half the sugar. Mix cornflour with remaining sugar and fold carefully into egg mix using a metal spoon. Fold in vinegar and essence, being careful not to flatten mixture. Spoon into prepared tin and bake in the slow oven for 45-50 mins., until firm outside but still soft inside. Invert tin gently upside-down onto a serving plate, and tip pavlova out. Remove paper and leave to cool — it will shrink a little during cooling. Do not decorate until ready to serve.

To serve — spread with whipped or Chantilly cream and arrange fruit on top, or sprinkle cream with chopped or flaked nuts or grated chocolate.

MERINGUES
Makes 4-6 meringue shells

Everyone thinks of meringues when needing to use up spare egg whites — what a lovely excuse for a treat, and they're so quick and easy to make as well. Unfilled meringue shells will keep crisp for weeks in an airtight tin or plastic box, so make them when you have spare egg whites and store ready to produce an impressive sweet at a moment's notice.

Preparation and cooking time: 1¾-2¼ hours

Each egg white will make 4 large or 6 small single meringue shells
For each egg white use 2 oz/50g sugar
Sandwich together with stiffly whipped cream — ¼ pt/150ml double cream will sandwich 8-12 meringues

Heat oven to 100°C/200°F/gas ¼-½. Line 1 or 2 large baking trays with silicone or oiled greaseproof paper — you can get 8-12 meringue shells on each tray. Use sandwich tins if you haven't enough trays.

Put egg whites into a large bowl and whisk with a whisk, mixer or processor until stiff and forming soft peaks. Continue whisking, adding the sugar a tsp at a time until it is all mixed in and meringue is thick, creamy and stiff; do not beat any more once all the sugar is in or the meringue will go flat. Use a tblsp to put meringue shapes onto the prepared trays, or if you want to be posh, put meringue carefully into a forcing bag with a large star tube, and pipe into shells, stars or rosettes.

Leave space between the meringues. Bake in the cool oven for 1½-2 hrs. according to size — the meringues should be pale but crisp and dry.

Remove from oven, cool for a few mins., then put carefully onto a wire tray and leave until quite cold. Store meringues in an airtight tin or plastic box, or use at once. Do not store meringues in the fridge, they go soft and weepy.

To serve — sandwich together with stiffly whipped cream, and arrange on a serving dish.

To make a flavoured cream, whip *1 tblsp* drinking chocolate or *1 tsp* instant coffee powder with the cream.

Sprinkle finished filled meringues with a few chopped nuts or flaked almonds if liked, or decorate with pieces of glacé cherries.

Chocolate Meringues: carefully fold 1 dsp drinking chocolate per egg white into the meringue mixture before spooning or piping meringue shapes. Sandwich meringues together when cold with chocolate-flavoured cream (see above).

Nutty Meringues: very gently fold 1 dsp chopped mixed nuts, chopped pistachio nuts or almond slivers into the meringue mixture before spooning or piping meringue shapes.

Sandwich cooked meringue shells together with whipped cream into which you have folded a tblsp chopped nuts or almond slivers (coffee-flavoured cream is delicious with the nuts).

Make an exotic instant dessert by sandwiching meringues together with a scoop of soft ice-cream (lots of lovely flavours are now available, choc chip, choc and toffee, mint chip, pineapple, etc.), and serving meringues in pretty sundae glasses decorated with whipped or aerosol cream and topping with fruit, nuts or grated chocolate. For a party buffet, serve a big bowl of tiny, unfilled meringues beside a big bowl of fresh strawberries or fruit salad and a bowl of whipped cream, and let the guests help themselves.

Meringue Nests or Crisp Pavlova: make meringue as above, but shape or pipe into small nest shapes or a large flan case (1 egg white will make 2 nests, a large pavlova will need 2 or 3 egg whites), bake until crisp in the slow oven and then cool on a wire tray. Fill with cream, ice-cream and fruit just before serving.

SUPER SUMMER PUDDING   *Serves 4-6*

Justify the cost of the thick cream which is marvellous with this pudding by economising on the dry bread and odds and ends of fruit from the garden or freezer. This pud is at its best when the beautiful soft fruits are in season — choose any mixture to produce the loveliest fresh, fruity taste imaginable. The hardest part of the preparation is persuading the bread slices to stay around the pudding basin to make a lining, and once you've done that the rest is so easy.

Make the day before eating and chill in the fridge for 24 hours.

Preparation and cooking time: 20 mins. plus overnight chilling time

2 lb/1kg mixed soft (traditionally red) fruit — choose from raspberries, strawberries, red- and blackcurrants, cherries, blackberries, etc.)

4-8 oz/100-225g sugar to taste

1 small loaf — traditionally white, but brown is nice too

To serve: **½ pt/300ml double cream or crème fraiche**

Keep different fruits separate. Pick over fruits, removing stems and stones, and rinse in cold water. Put sugar into a large pan, and, starting with the fruit which needs most cooking (e.g.

currants, blackberries, cherries) put wet fruit into pan with the sugar and simmer over a *very* gentle heat for 3-4 mins., stirring carefully until the sugar melts and the fruit juices run. Add the rest of the fruit and cook gently for a further minute or two until all the fruit is just soft. Do not overcook, the fruit should remain whole.

Slice bread into thin slices — ¼"/½cm thick. Cut off crusts and line base and sides of 1½ pt/900ml pudding basin artistically with slices of bread, moulding the bread to close the gaps and filling in any little holes with bread patches. Pour hot fruit and juice into mould, saving a little juice, and cover with a bread lid. Pinch all the edges together. Find a small saucer, plate or lid that will fit inside the basin and put it on the bread lid. Weigh the whole thing down with a weight (I don't have one, so I usually balance a big jar of jam or a tin of syrup on top.) Leave in fridge overnight.

To serve: Remove weight and plate and carefully unmould pud onto a large serving dish (put dish over basin, turn the lot upside-down, shake gently and remove basin) to reveal a glorious red summer pudding. Paint any white patches with the reserved juice and pour the rest over the pud. Serve cold with dollops of thick cream or crème fraiche.

FRUIT FOOL   *Serves 4*

A gorgeous pud, so quick and simple to make, yet served in a pretty glass it looks as good as the most sophisticated dessert. This is a good way of dealing with a glut of fruit from the garden or over zealous labours at the 'pick your own' farm!

Preparation and cooking time: 10-30 mins., depending on type of fruit

Use 1 lb/500g fresh fruit to ½ pt/300ml cream, so for 4
   servings use 1 lb/500g fruit — strawberries, raspberries,
   gooseberries, blackberries, etc.
Sugar to taste — 2-4 oz/50-100g approx. according to type
   of fruit
½ pt/300ml double cream
Fresh fruit or chopped nuts to decorate (optional)

Prepare and purée fruit according to kind:
Strawberries and raspberries — wash, drain and mash gently.
Gooseberries and blackberries — wash, put into a pan with
   2 tblsp water and simmer for 8-10 mins. until soft.
   Liquidise or process, then sieve to produce a velvety smooth
   purée.
   Sweeten fruit with sugar to taste. Whip cream until thick but
not solid and fold into fruit purée. Pour into a serving dish or
individual glasses and chill before serving. Decorate with fresh
fruit or a sprinkle of nuts and serve with shortbread or a posh
wafer biscuit.
   This fool is a very rich mixture. For a lighter pudding or to
make it go further (serve 4-6 people), whip 1 or 2 egg whites
until stiff and fold into the fruit and cream mixture before putting
it into the serving dish. This really is an instant pud if you
already have prepared fruit purée in the freezer; just defrost
and mix with the whipped cream and serve.

QUICK FRUITY ICE-CREAM

Make the mousse (either mixture) as above, and pour it into a
shallow plastic container and freeze. After about an hour, when
nearly frozen, turn it into a basin and beat to break up the ice
crystals. Pour back into the container and freeze until needed.

Take container from freezer half an hour before using and allow the ice-cream to soften before use.

KI'S APPLE SNOW   *Serves 4*

A 'cream-less fruit fool', ideal for slimmers or those, like Ki (my youngest son), who dislike cream. Very cheap, very light and very quick to make. Use up windfall apples or pre-prepared apple purée later in the year.

Preparation and cooking time: 10-25 mins.

1 lb/500g cooking apples
2 tblsp water, white wine or cider
1 tblsp lemon juice or half a lemon
2-4 oz/50-100g sugar to taste
2 egg whites

Make apple purée — peel, core and slice apples, simmer gently in a pan with water, wine or cider and lemon juice. If using a lemon, pare the yellow skin and simmer that with the fruit. When soft (5-10 mins.), purée apple (remove lemon peel first), using a liquidiser or processor or mash with a fork. Sweeten to taste and leave to cool. Whip egg whites until stiff and fold into the apple. Pile into a serving bowl or individual dishes and chill. Serve the same day, as it separates if left too long.

MELON AND CITRUS SORBET   *Serves 4-6*

A very light water ice with a refreshing flavour, lovely on a warm day or to serve between courses at a smart dinner party.

Preparation and cooking time: 20 mins. plus approx. 4 hrs. freezing time

1 ripe honeydew melon
Rind and juice of 1 orange
Rind and juice of 1 lemon
8-12 oz/200-300g sugar
½ pt/300ml water
2 egg whites

Cut melon in half, scoop out seeds, remove flesh into a saucepan and mash with a fork or potato masher. Add orange and lemon rind and juices, sugar to taste and water, stir well. Bring to the boil over a moderate heat, reduce heat and simmer for 5-10 mins. until melon is soft. Pour into a shallow plastic tray, leave to cool and then freeze until semi-frozen (about an hour). Tip into a bowl and break up with a fork, then mash well to break up the ice crystals.

Beat egg whites until stiff and fold gently into melon mixture Pour back into plastic tray and freeze again until hard, approx. 2-3 hours.

Remove from freezer 15-20 mins. before serving to allow ice to soften slightly. Serve scoops of sorbet in pretty glasses, decorated with a tiny sprig of mint leaves or lemon balm.

ST. CLEMENT'S DESSERT   *Serves 4*

Well scrub 4 oranges or large lemons, cut 'lids' off the tops and scoop out all the fruit and juice (some may be used in the sorbet, eat the rest or save the juice for cooking later). Prepare Melon Sorbet as above, but after folding in the egg white, spoon sorbet into prepared fruit, pop on the lids, wrap in cling film and freeze upright for 2-3 hours. Allow to soften for 15-20 mins. before serving.

SOFT CHANTILLY CREAM

Makes ½ pt/300ml

Adding the whisked egg white to the whipped cream makes it go twice as far (useful if you have unexpected guests!) and produces a lovely light cream, often appreciated with a rich dessert after a heavy meal, particularly at Christmas time.

Preparation time: 5 mins.

1 egg white
¼ pt/150ml whipping cream or ¼ pt/150ml double cream
  with 2 tblsp single cream or top of the milk
2 tsp caster or icing sugar (this may be omitted if you find
  it too sweet)
Few drops vanilla essence

Whip egg white until stiff but not dry. Without washing the whisk, whip the chosen cream until thick, then mix in sugar and vanilla essence to taste. Fold in beaten egg white and heap cream into a pretty serving dish. Keep in fridge until ready to serve.

   (If you whip the cream first, remember to wash the whisk before beating the egg white, or it will not stiffen.)

CRUNCHY BISCUIT BASE

8-9"/20-22cm base

Use up odds and ends of biscuits to make a base for your favourite cheesecake recipe or a meringue pie. Any mixture of plain, cream or chocolate that has accumulated in the biscuit tin — usually the 'unpopular' varieties from the mixed packets. Top up weight with plain or chocolate digestives.

Preparation time: 5 mins.

6 oz/150g biscuits
3 oz/75g butter
2 oz/50g demerara sugar

Put biscuits into a large bowl and crush with the end of a rolling pin. Put butter into a saucepan and melt over a very gentle heat (do not let it boil or brown), or melt in a microwave oven, stir in biscuit crumbs and sugar. Butter the base and sides of a loose bottomed or spring clip flan ring or a pottery flan dish, and spread mixture evenly over dish.

When cool, cover with chosen topping and bake or leave to set according to topping recipe.

JON JON'S TAKE BACK CHOCOLATE BISCUIT CAKE

A favourite of my middle son. It's ideal to take back to school, college or your own flat after a weekend at home. Use up any mixture of leftover biscuits, plain or cream, and add some dried fruit if you wish, which results in a softer, chewier cake.

Preparation time: 20 mins. plus cooling time

8 oz/225g biscuits — digestives (plain or chocolate), or any mixture
4 oz/100g butter or hard margarine
2 heaped tblsp sugar
2 tsp cocoa or 4 tsp drinking chocolate
1 tblsp golden syrup or honey
2 oz/50g sultanas or seedless raisins (optional)
4 oz/100g chocolate cake covering or cooking chocolate

Well butter a shallow baking tin (round or square), approximately 8"/20cm in diameter. Put chosen biscuits into a deep bowl and crush them (not too finely), with the end of a rolling pin. Put butter, sugar, cocoa or drinking chocolate and syrup or honey into a pan and melt slowly over a low heat until runny, stirring occasionally. Remove from heat, stir in crushed biscuits and dried fruit if used, mix well. Tip into prepared tin, spread flat and leave for a few minutes to cool.

Melt chocolate or cake covering in a heat-proof basin in a saucepan with 1"/2½cm hot water, over a very low heat, then pour chocolate over cake, spread smoothly with a swirly pattern and leave to set in a cool place. Cut into small squares (everyone will take two pieces!) and store in an airtight tin or plastic box.

I usually make double quantity as this cake is always so popular, and use a large Swiss roll tin. The cake can be cut into squares and frozen.

YUMMY BANANA BREAD

Use up the soft, ripe bananas that are left in the fruit bowl. Eat this bread on its own or spread with butter.

Preparation and cooking time: 1¼-1½ hours

4 oz/100g soft margarine
4 oz/100g sugar
8 oz/225g self raising flour
½ tsp baking powder
Pinch salt
2 eggs
3-4 bananas (according to size)
Grated rind of 1 orange and lemon
or ½ tsp mixed spice
4 oz/100g mixed dried fruit (optional)

Heat oven to 150°C/300°F/gas 2-3. Well grease a 2 lb/1kg loaf tin and line the base with greased greaseproof paper. Put margarine and sugar into a mixing bowl or processor. Sieve flour, baking powder and salt into the bowl, add the eggs and beat well with an electric mixer or processor (you can use a wooden spoon but it's hard work and takes longer!). Slice bananas into a basin and mash with a fork or potato masher, then add to the cake mixture, grate in orange or lemon rind and beat again until well mixed. Stir in washed dried fruit, if used, and spice, and mix well. Pour mixture into greased tin and bake in the low oven for about an hour until well risen and firm to the touch. Cool in the tin for a few minutes, then turn onto a wire tray, remove paper and leave until cold.

Serve on its own or with butter, or, if you're really self-indulgent, with butter and apricot jam.

INDEX

More Cookery Books by Jan Arkless

HOW TO BOIL AN EGG
Simple Cookery for One

An ideal companion for those who have never previously had to cook for themselves. Jan shows how to produce good, nourishing, interesting meals for one, without the problems of trying to adapt family-size recipes. Written for those people who are suddenly faced with having to cook for themselves, perhaps after years of being looked after, it's also the perfect *entrée* for youngsters leaving home for the first time.

NO MEAT FOR ME, PLEASE!
Recipes for the Vegetarian in the Family

This book contains a wealth of good advice and sumptuous recipes for the busy cook who has a vegetarian in the family. The recipe instructions are mostly given in quantities suitable for a single portion so that the book is also of value to the vegetarian who lives alone.

THE DINNER PARTY PLANNER

Full of recipes and helpful hints on menu planning and advanced preparation for a successful dinner party. Contains suggested menus which show how to select individual dishes and combine them to create a delicious easy-to-prepare meal.

Uniform with this book

OUR PUBLISHING POLICY

HOW WE CHOOSE

Our policy is to consider every deserving manuscript and we can give special editorial help where an author is an authority on his subject but an inexperienced writer. We are rigorously selective in the choice of books we publish. We set the highest standards of editorial quality and accuracy. This means that a *Paperfront* is easy to understand and delightful to read. Where illustrations are necessary to convey points of detail, these are drawn up by a subject specialist artist from our panel.

HOW WE KEEP PRICES LOW

We aim for the big seller. This enables us to order enormous print runs and achieve the lowest price for you. Unfortunately, this means that you will not find in the *Paperfront* list any titles on obscure subjects of minority interest only. These could not be printed in large enough quantities to be sold for the low price at which we offer this series.

We sell almost all our *Paperfronts* at the same unit price. This saves a lot of fiddling about in our clerical departments and helps us to give you world-beating value. Under this system, the longest titles are offered at a price which we believe to be unmatched by any publisher in the world.

OUR DISTRIBUTION SYSTEM

Because of the competitive price, and the rapid turnover, *Paperfronts* are possibly the most profitable line a bookseller can handle. They are stocked by the best bookshops all over the world. It may be that your bookseller has run out of stock of a particular title. If so, he can order more from us at any time—we have a fine reputation for "same day" despatch, and we supply any order, however small (even a single copy), to any bookseller who has an account with us. We prefer you to buy from your bookseller, as this reminds him of the strong underlying public demand for *Paperfronts*. Members of the public who live in remote places, or who are housebound, or whose local bookseller is unco-operative, can order direct from us by post.

FREE

If you would like an up-to-date list of all *Paperfront* titles currently available, send a stamped self-addressed envelope to
ELLIOT RIGHT WAY BOOKS, BRIGHTON RD.,
LOWER KINGSWOOD, SURREY, UK.